DIRECT SELLING 101

In signature Vicki Fitch style, *Direct Selling 101* is a book that clearly covers sales, but it is so much more. It is a roadmap (or island map) to becoming the best version of yourself. She brilliantly blended all the principles of building a business with common sense, insightful analogies, and of course the **Fitchtionary**. This book is an easy read and a sure indication that the future volumes will be a **must have** resource on every entrepreneur's bookshelf.

– **Joel Comm**, New York Times Best Selling Author

Vicki Fitch lays it out in a no-nonsense approach to direct selling. She incorporates personality, engagement, hard work, relationship building, and developing your own personal style… just like what she demonstrates in everything she takes on. She always shines like a beacon of positivity. Vicki totally "gets" two things I have always built my business around… Relationships are like muscle tissue; the more you engage them, the stronger and more valuable they become, AND… A Network gives you reach, but a Community gives you Power. If you want to make a difference as a direct seller, or in any business you take on, don't miss this book.

– **Ted Rubin**, Social Marketing Strategist, Photofy CMO/Advisor, MC/Host Brand Innovator Summits

Don't let the title fool you! Yes, *Direct Selling 101* will help you develop foundational skills to sell successfully—but the real power in this book is that it will build your confidence and help you shed the fears and excuses that are holding you back from achieving your Dreams. Success is possible, and Vicki will lead you down the path to Success Island and help you navigate any pitfalls along the way. If you let her… Because if you take away just one thing from this book—know this: with the right mindset and the right mentor, anything is possible!

– **Shannon Mattern**, Website Developer and owner of WP-BFF

This book is so good I couldn't put it down! I am not in Direct Sales, but this book makes me want to go out there and join the industry! Vicki is amazing at what she does. The idea of selling is very scary for me, but *Direct Selling 101* is so full of helpful information that after reading this book, I am full of confidence that I would be good at it! She blended in funny stories which made me laugh, and she gave me hope. I really enjoyed reading this and I highly recommend it! I will read this over and over again and I am so excited to read the rest of the series!

— **Dorothy Boyd**, Chapel Hill, North Carolina

Learning more about direct selling was a given. Being *inspired* to take action via the lessons and step-by-step processes outlined in the book was an unexpected revelation.

— **Aaron Roth**, VP Sales & Marketing, Arkon Mounts

If direct sales has ever scared you, then this book will equip you with the confidence you'll need to make all the sales you want to succeed in your business. *Direct Selling 101* is the book that I will go back to over and over again because it is literally thousands of dollars' worth of sales coaching and knowledge of people, put skillfully and humorously into bite-size pieces that anyone can digest. Vicki has hit it out of the park with this book and I can't wait to read the rest of her series.

— **Stacy Lynn Harp**, Bible News Radio

Genius! This book is so intelligently written, and it covers so many topics that I was left wanting *Direct Selling 201* tomorrow! What more is Vicki going to teach us in the next 11 volumes? *"Just out of curiosity…"*

— **Jan Turley**, OBR Merino, New Zealand

Vicki Fitch's *Direct Selling 101* book was incredible! I read it in one sitting and was impressed with all of the takeaways I could immediately implement for my business. It's not just for people in direct sales—it's for ANYONE in business! Not only was her book full of useful strategies and resources, but Vicki's unique way of writing about the sales journey kept me engaged (and laughing!) the entire time. I highly recommend *Direct Selling 101*!

— **Leisa Reid**, Founder of Get Speaking Gigs Now

Good stuff Vicki! Great format! Easy read! Jam packed with great knowledge! … you can quote me!

— **Nyra Carranza**, Direct Sales Industry Consultant

Vicki Fitch's writing style is fun and entertaining, and she gives you great visuals so that you can envision what you need to be doing in business. She has created a land with different islands, paths, and modes of transportation that take you on a journey with her as she teaches and shares her experiences. I am not in the direct sales business, but I AM in business—a new entrepreneur. Her book is for anyone who wants to learn about business and can use encouragement along the way (can't we all?). I highly recommend you get this book, and I am looking forward to her next books, too.

– **Judy Peacock**, Peacock Country Travel

DIRECT SELLING
101

The Step by Step Guide to
#RockThatDream
in the Direct Sales Industry

VICKI FITCH

NEW YORK

LONDON • NASHVILLE • MELBOURNE • VANCOUVER

DIRECT SELLING 101
The Step by Step Guide to #RockThatDream in the Direct Sales Industry

© 2019 **VICKI FITCH**

Published in New York, New York, by Morgan James Publishing. Morgan James is a trademark of Morgan James, LLC. www.MorganJamesPublishing.com

ISBN 978-1-64279-007-8 paperback
ISBN 978-1-64279-008-5 eBook
Library of Congress Control Number: 2018935829

Original Cover concept by:
Jay McKey
www.JayMcKey.com

Cover Design by:
Rachel Lopez
www.r2cdesign.com

In an effort to support local communities, raise awareness and funds, Morgan James Publishing donates a percentage of all book sales for the life of each book to Habitat for Humanity Peninsula and Greater Williamsburg.

Get involved today! Visit
www.MorganJamesBuilds.com

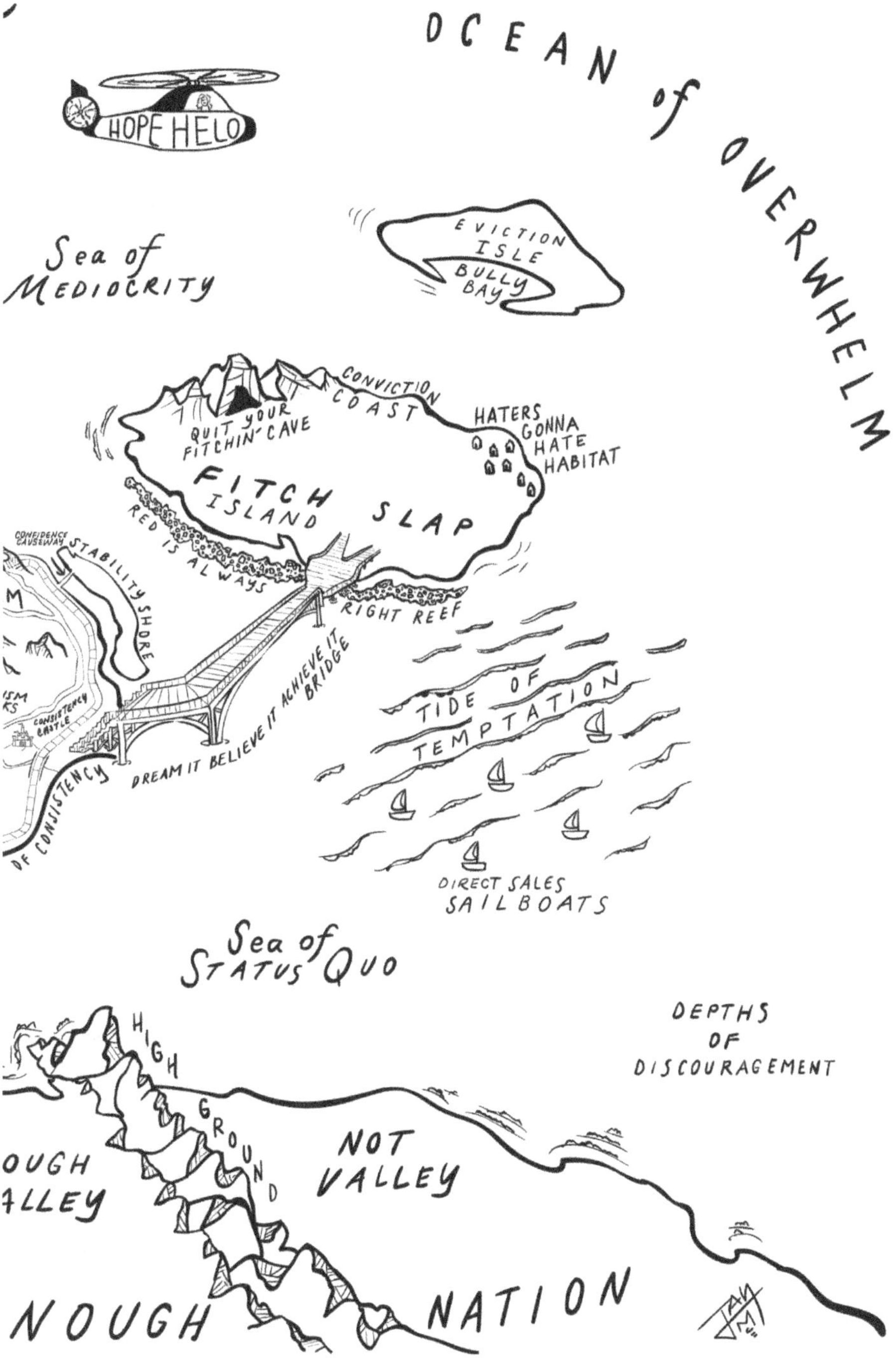
OCEAN of OVERWHELM
HOPE HELO
Sea of Mediocrity
EVICTION ISLE
BULLY BAY
CONVICTION COAST
QUIT YOUR FITCHIN' CAVE
HATERS GONNA HATE HABITAT
FITCH ISLAND
SLAP
RED IS ALWAYS RIGHT REEF
CONFIDENCE CAUSEWAY
STABILITY SHORE
CONSISTENCY CASTLE
DREAM IT BELIEVE IT ACHIEVE IT BRIDGE
OF CONSISTENCY
TIDE OF TEMPTATION
DIRECT SALES SAILBOATS
Sea of Status Quo
DEPTHS OF DISCOURAGEMENT
HIGH GROUND
NOT VALLEY
OUGH ALLEY
NOUGH NATION

DEDICATION

Just as this **#12Books12Months** series isn't typical, neither is my dedication page. If you haven't already, you will learn that I am a bit unconventional.

First, this book is dedicated **to my family**.

To my husband **Terry** for being my biggest admirer and for singing my praises to anyone who will listen. You introduced me to the great sales and motivational trainers like Jim Rohn and Tom Hopkins, which started a lifelong love of learning and reaching for my **Dreams.** You reminded me to take those leaps of faith in myself and helped me to become the leader I am today. Your brilliant marketing mind and your commitment to connecting with people continues to inspire me and remind me what a wonderful couple we are, melding our talents to share with others. Thank you for being a Godly man, a fabulous father, and my best friend. I love you with all my heart.

To my oldest son **Zach**, for recognizing the value of the entrepreneurial spirit and supporting me in my **Dream** of writing this entire **#12Books12Months** series. I love watching you and your business grow as you graciously allow me to give you input. My favorite part is watching the amazing young man you've become. Your commitment to our family is unyielding and I see so much of myself in you. I love you, *"Higher than the mountains…"*

To my youngest son **Elijah**, for being my inspiration to see others for all they are. For helping me to hone my communication skills and to always look at situations from a different perspective. I love your out-of-the-box thinking style and willingness to learn. Thank you for actually reading my books! (Even though it was assigned reading, I know we learned a lot together!) I love the way you see the world and how you have helped me grow as a person! **#QuirkyIsCool**.

I couldn't have done any of this without all of you, and I am forever grateful for our Fitch Family Motto:

Fitch's Never Give Up!

Secondly, to all the entrepreneurs out there who are not only bold enough to venture into business, but brave enough to become the best version of themselves, in business and in life… this book is for you.

TABLE OF CONTENTS

FOREWORD

My mission is to rid the world of "salesy weirdos", so I spend most of my time helping people be more human in the way they sell—whether it's examining how they communicate face to face in their conversations, removing the crazy amount of exclamations in their emails, or simply understanding human behavior to connect faster. We all know what it feels like to be sold to by an amateur. And if you've ever tried to sell anything, you know that icky feeling you get when you become what you didn't want to. That's the "salesy weirdo."

As I travel around the world, speaking, coaching, and consulting on sales, I get the pleasure of meeting amazing people who are out there making an impact in their customers' lives. I've coached and consulted with billion-dollar multinationals, entrepreneurs, and startups in countless industries. It doesn't matter what you sell; it's all about humans. I've learned that most of us are somewhat weird already. Being a salesy weirdo just means that you tried to be someone else. Embrace your weirdness and be real. Be authentic, have fun with your customers, and love selling.

The best part is that I love meeting weirdos!

These are the unique humans making a real impact on those around them. When I met Vicki Fitch, I think my search for the best weirdo of all was complete. She is someone who has her own thirteen-page dictionary to help you understand all the interesting terms she uses. She is a powerful woman who stubbornly goes and wins despite others telling her, that they may be crazy ideas.

I was introduced to Vicki through a friend about being a guest on her podcast. We met on a video call to connect and ended up talking for over three hours. We had to almost have someone separate us from each other. Why? Well, we have very similar values and vision when it comes to selling. We both believe that you need to put in the right work and plan well to go after those BHAGs. We know that most success happens when others aren't looking, so you have to find a way to have joy in the mundane. To be successful in sales, your number one commitment must be the happiness of your customer, and you will need to work like a maniac to understand how to serve them. We both understand the pressure of being positive and enthusiastic while there are fires raging all around you. All of this while having fun and making it look easy, so others can be empowered to win.

I was so excited when Vicki told me she was writing these books because I know how much knowledge, real world experience, and time she has put into turning what she intuitively knows into an absolute resource that anyone can follow—regardless of experience. Back in the day, when I was doing direct selling, I would have killed to get my hands-on Vicki's work. Where were you then, Vicki?

As you read through the book, pay close attention to the subtle language she uses. The stories are powerful examples of real scenarios that you can learn from and apply today in your own business. They will help you get an edge. Vicki shares some killer tips for hosting your own events in direct selling, like making the pre-class calls yourself instead of your hostess or brand-new consultant. When you read that section, look at how effortless the process seems. That is the mark of an expert—someone who makes it look easy because all the details make sense. Implement these ideas word for word. Likewise, when Vicki helps you visualize Rejection Ridge as a very short distance to travel to get you to the road you are seeking, she helps you recognize that it just **looks** scary. So, when she helps you understand the need to create a market separator to have people chasing you to come to your events because it sounds like a ton of fun to them—stop there and take notes.

If you are serious about growing your business, as a professional, and as a human, then you're in the right place. In sales, you need to have the right skillset, toolset, and mindset to go after your goals. The journey should always be one of constant improvement. Courses, books, mentors, coaches, and resources are out there for you to grow through. Make the most of them by applying one lesson at a time until it becomes a part of your DNA. If you take one idea for the next month and absolutely nail it, imagine what you can accomplish in five years if you just did that every month. SIXTY new skill sets will be a part of your new reality.

We all want that homerun and instant success. The real winners are the ones who do the hard work to make the rest look easy. Year after year. Put the time into these resources and you will be rewarded.

I was thrilled when Vicki asked me to write this foreword as I know how much she has done for her audience, her clients, and her family through her work. I feel honored to be a part of her journey, and now yours, through this book. Go take action, serve your customers, and achieve your dreams. Have fun and don't be a salesy weirdo.

—**Joe Girard,** Sales Leadership and Performance Coach,
Change Grow Achieve

ACKNOWLEDGMENTS

I want to start by acknowledging my husband **Terry**, who has always shown his **Belief** in me and my **Dreams**. He has been there through the ups and downs, including me spending 3 ½ years in a wheelchair, which was no picnic. Not to mention the dedication it took for me to do this **#12Books12Months** project and the extra responsibilities he took on when I got behind because I was sick for three months! He comedically refers to himself as "Vicki's husband" at any event we attend, and is always the first to brag about how talented and amazing I am. I couldn't have asked for a better man in my life or a stronger partner. Thank you honey, for being my biggest fan, my most avid supporter, and for being someone who reminds me (and everyone else) that **#IAmEnough**.

I also need to thank my children **Zach** and **Elijah,** who were the inspiration for many of the stories and situations expressed. They have been supportive by providing their opinions, helping me clarify points, and even finding a couple type-o's! You two boys are why I do what I do. I want to share the **#YouAreEnough** mission with the world, and knowing that you two **Believe** in me and that you are willing to help me achieve my **Dreams** means the world to me.

Things wouldn't be complete without thanking my step-children, **Jason** and **Tera,** who have been along for this wild ride as well. Besides the personal joy they brought to the relationship, they have expanded our lovely family. First, by adding on their spouses, **Erika** and **Mitchel**, and then blessing us with five amazing grandchildren. Some of them you have seen on my **Livestreams**. **Olivia**, **Jack**, **Ben**, **Andrew** and **Taylor**, I adore you all and I appreciate each of you for the unique personalities you have, and all that you have brought to my life. You may be showing up in some of the future books!

Since we are talking about family, a big thank you to my sister **Susan** who believed in me and my vision to own a home as a teenager. She pulled together her hard-earned tips and savings to make my **Dream** our reality. She also taught me how to drive, but that is a story for another book!

If you have **that** friend who knows everything about you, and you want to make sure it stays secretly locked away in the recesses of their mind, you better acknowledge them in your book! **Kathy Jean**, you are one crazy girl who has kept me on my toes for longer than I care to admit I've been alive. (I'm only 22 of course!) You will make your debut later in the series, but the length of time we've been friends alone warrants an honorable mention. Now, just keep quiet about… everything!

Next, I want to thank my dear friend **Erin Cell**. We got a chance to really connect when I spoke at her **Social Media Day Denver** conference in 2017. I love her heart and her desire to help other people. It was her involvement in one of my **Livestreams**, where I shared my **#BHAG** of the **#12Books12Months** project, that sparked her immediate support and the virtual introduction to **David Hancock** of **Morgan James Publishing**.

David, thank you for believing in me, my crazy **#BHAG,** and the commitment behind this **#12Books12Months** project and the **#YouAreEnough** campaign that I plan to take global. Recognizing the value in others is something I enjoy doing, but it is incredibly satisfying when someone is willing to Step Up and do the same for me. I experienced that from our first conversation, and I hope you know I am even more appreciative of you and your team today than I was then. You work with exceptional people and I am honored to be part of the **Morgan James Publishing** family.

Since we are talking about **Morgan James Publishing**, I must thank the staff members that have been assigned to work with me. I feel a bit sorry for them with my never-ending list of questions on how to make this process as easy as possible. By the time the twelfth book in the series is done, I imagine I will be a seasoned pro, but the first one is always the toughest. Thank you, **Aubrey**, for getting the process started and to **Margo** for understanding and working with me through those 3 months of illness that put the project behind. Thank you to the rest of the team as well. Without all of you, none of this would have been possible. We have a lot more work to do, so no rest for you! You've got more manuscripts to review!

To my team, **Iris** for editing so many manuscripts that she could probably write my next book for me! To **CeeCee** and **Yanna** for trying to keep up with me, my energy, and the fast pace we try to get things done!

To my amazing illustrator **Jay McKey,** who has the unbelievable ability to listen to the words I say and somehow draw them on paper. I love how patient he is with all the things I add to **Fitchipelago**, and how he is willing to modify or add new drawings when I need them. He is an outstanding talent and I am so blessed to be working with him!

To my dear friend **Joe Girard** who, after reading the book, volunteered to do the Foreword and helped me adjust a few things to give them more impact. That includes changing the **Fitchisms and More Dictionary** to the perfectly titled **Fitchtionary**. (I should have thought of that myself!) When you have people like Joe in your corner, sharing **#TruthBombs** with you while encouraging your progress, it makes the journey that much richer. Thank you for your insight **Joe** and for remembering **#RedIsAlwaysRight**. (You will find out more about what that means in another book!)

The last group of people I need to thank, starts with my first upline **Kathi Hollingsworth**, who offered me the gift of being in the Direct Sales Industry. That one simple question she asked me changed the trajectory of my life. Thank you, **Kathi**, for having the courage to ask a very busy entrepreneur to join you on your journey. I **Believe** this book, and that story, will inspire others in the industry to reach out, face their **FEAR,** and **#RockThatDream**.

There is a long list of people over the years who inspired me. You will meet many of them in other books in the series, so I will thank them in the books where they are mentioned. **Nyra Carranza** was one of my first mentors in Direct Sales. Her bright and sunny disposition, even when things were tough, helped me stay focused on my **Bright Side** philosophy. I was blessed to reconnect with her on LinkedIn after many years, by sharing a copy of this book with her and thanking her for the difference she made in my life. Another reminder of the power of **Social Media** and why you need to make sure you are using it!

Another group I must thank is my **#Fitch5000 Tribe**. They have supported me and this project from the beginning and reminded me when things get tricky, like being sick for three months, that I was not alone. They kept praying for me, messaging me, encouraging me, and reminding me that my message was important and that they would wait patiently for the results. Although they are listed in the back of this book, I have highlighted a few individuals who have gone above and beyond, supporting me and my efforts.

This group of amazing people jumped on tasks the moment I asked. Some volunteered to review specific parts of the book, the entire book, or just give me clarity when my mind was fading. They spent their time and energy reminding me that my content was valuable, and that the world needed what I had to offer.

Stacy Lynn Harp, if there was a president of my fan club, I think that would have to be you. Always rallying, supporting, encouraging, interviewing, connecting, reading, editing, and communicating with the **Tribe**. Helping to keep my **Dream** alive by joining my **Livestreams** and sharing them out on a regular basis, reminding me that I was human, (I forget sometimes LOL) and that you **Believe** in me and my **Dream**. Thank you for all you do. A big thank you to your wonderful husband **Randall Harp** too, who is always ready for an intellectual debate on things that matter, including the word "impactful". That word will forever be stuck in my mind as will his **#Goodbye** video. I may have to put that on the resources page for this book!

Lisa Sulsenti for pre-editing the first manuscript without knowing how to use the tracking feature in Word. Here's to the hours you put in and the good laugh we had later.

Dotty, Melanie, Claudia, Lisa, Judy, Marsha, and **Shannon**, thank you for reading and providing your input and for participating and sharing out my content and engaging in my **Livestreams. David, Anna, Jeremy, Adam & Adam (Adam Squared)**, and **Stacy, Stacy & Stacey (Stacy Cubed)** I must thank you all as well because you have all been avid supporters.

My life is more complete having all of you in it. You have made a difference in my life and the enthusiasm in which I share my message. I hope and pray that I have provided as much value to all of you, as you have to me. Thank you for being part of my **Tribe**. I am forever grateful.

I would also like to acknowledge my parents, **Henry & Joan Hainault**. I am so sad that they are not here to see this project come to fruition, but I am confident that they would both have been very proud.

Although you will see through this **#12Books12Months** journey that my younger years were not the happiest times in my life, I grew to understand my parents, their love for me, and the sometimes unique way they showed it. They taught me so very much, including how to have a strong work ethic, how to find a solution to my problems and, sometimes to their chagrin, how to have the **Determination** to achieve the things that others said I couldn't.

They weren't perfect parents, and I wasn't a perfect child, but the Bible reminds us in Ecclesiastes that God makes everything beautiful in **His** time. I **Believe** the culmination of my life experience has blossomed and is truly beautiful. I pray that the world would see that in my actions every day.

The final and yet most important acknowledgement goes to my Lord and Savior, **Jesus Christ**. He is my **Rock** and the foundation in which all these principles are based on. My ability to articulate these ideas to you is strictly because He found favor in me and gave me the gift of expressing myself, as well as understanding others. My life, who I am, and everything I have done, are all for the Glory of God. I am truly humbled and privileged to be His servant. He is the one that inspired me to **#RockThatDream**.

Introduction

READ ME FIRST!

The journey we are about to take together is one that can change your life forever. It is my sincere desire that when you read this series, it will inspire you to become all that you can be. Each of the twelve books can stand alone and deliver value on their particular topic. But as a whole, all twelve books build on each other, inviting and encouraging you to grow in amazing ways. The **#12Books12Months** series will seamlessly provide a place for you to develop your **Confidence**, character, and community, while turning your passion into your profits. I hope you will trust me when I tell you that this will be a life-changing experience. There is no need do it alone! Invite your friends to **#JoinTheJourney**. It's time to live the life of your **Dreams**.

The inside cover of this book is a map to navigate your way around **Fitchipelago**. In case you aren't familiar, an **archipelago** is a sea or stretch of water containing many islands. **Fitchipelago** encompasses the numerous islands and bodies of water that are depicted in my books. I want to help you successfully navigate the rough waters of life and business, so you can end up in the ultimate destination of **Success Island**.

If you are new to me, you may not know about my **#BHAG (Big Hairy Audacious Goal)** of publishing **#12Books12Months**. Many think I am crazy, but that is what a **#BHAG** is—a goal that is so big, it seems out of reach.

If you KNOW you can achieve it, it isn't a BHAG.

The map will help you understand how each of the books are connected. I have put the titles of future books in *Bold & Italics* to give you a precursor of what is coming ahead. All of them are part of the **M3 Philosophy (Money, Mindset & Motivation)** and will provide you with clearly defined, actionable steps to guide you on your journey.

You will learn to overcome the **Ocean of Overwhelm**, defy the **Depths of Discouragement**, and sail through the **Sea of Status Quo** on your way to **Success Island**. It will be my privilege to lead you to the **Pinnacle of Peace** on **#RockThatDream Ridge,** where you will have a 360-degree view of your future.

I promise to make you laugh, and maybe cry, because my journey has not always been fun. It's also been painful and frightening at times, but I made it through, and you will too.

I have always found humor to be a great way to communicate and I use a lot of my own lingo I call **Fitchisms**. I'm confident that my unique vocabulary will **Edutain (Edu**cate and Enter**tain)** you. This creative dictionary provides easy access to the terms I use and the often-humorous meanings behind them. I trust you will come to love and embrace them, like my existing **Friends, Followers,** and **Fans** already have.

For easy reference, I have included them in the **Fitchtionary** in the back of this book and added map locations, industry terms, specialty hashtags, and words or phrases that might not be widely-recognized by different cultures. I have tried to **bold** them throughout the text to make them easier to identify.

Many people wonder why I am taking on such a huge project in such a short period of time, so I wanted to clarify a couple of things. I did not decide to do this because I had something to prove, nor am I sacrificing quality for quantity.

I took on this #BHAG because the world needs Hope.

I started **Livestreaming** several years ago and I quickly attracted an audience of people who resonated with my unique, heartfelt, but "tell it like it is" style. During those daily broadcasts, I recognized the same struggles and questions over and over and made it a point to create fun analogies to help educate and empower the audience.

My consultations became very popular and as the questionnaires poured in, I noticed another pattern emerging. People across the globe were struggling to **Believe** in themselves, their talents, and their businesses. No matter what state, country, or province, the recurring theme was the same. There was a "**Bully**" in their heads who was repeatedly lying to them by telling them they were "Not Enough".

Some were discouraged, and some felt defeated. Helping them recognize their personal value became my mission. My success in business was the catalyst for some; recognizing the extensive trials I had overcome provided **Hope** for others. The same foundational principles are needed in life and business, so these books are a compilation of those principles.

- We all need to "sell" ourselves to others to be respected in our communities.
- We all need to "recruit" others to complete projects or tasks.
- We all need to "lead" people who are watching and learning from us.
- We all need to "connect" with others to find those who appreciate who we are.
- We all need to "market" our skills to the world in public and private.
- We all need to "brand" ourselves, personally and in business.
- We all need to accept that technology can be used to help or to hinder.
- We all need to **Believe** in ourselves, so we can withstand life's challenges.
- We all need to appreciate others for who they are and not who we want them to be.
- We all need to seek to grow and become the best version of ourselves.

- We all need to recognize that **Social Media** is a method of communicating and that leveraging the power of **Livestreaming** is powerful.
- We all need to understand that we will have difficult times and it is not what happens to us, but the way we handle them, that defines who we are.

Even if you think one title may not apply to you because you aren't in "sales" or you don't use **Social Media**, I promise you will learn something valuable in every book. The principles, analogies, and stories in each one will inspire you to understand others and increase your desire to be the best YOU, you can be.

Every title in this **#12Books12Months** series will add an additional layer of support to help you grow and learn, because we know there is always room for improvement. That is incredibly different from wanting to change because you don't **Believe** you are worthy or that you are under the false assumption that you are Not Good Enough. Remember, **#YouAreEnough** just the way you are.

Having a **Tribe** of people who **Believe** in you and your journey makes it easier and improves your chances for success. For that reason, I am inviting you to be part of our **Tribe**, the **#Fitch5000**. You will see a section in the back of each book listing these steadfast supporters who have helped me take this from a **#BHAG** in my head, to a reality. They are also helping me expand the **#YouAreEnough** global campaign into schools, corporations, and homes across the world.

If you would like to **#JoinTheJourney** and be part of the **#Fitch5000**, go to **www.VickiFitch.com/5K**. We will add your name to the back of a future book and who knows, if you participate in the group, you may get an acknowledgement, a thank you, or even a character named after you!

In closing, I want you to know that I am honored that you are reading this book. In an effort to make your journey even easier, I have provided you with a lot of additional resources at **www.VickiFitch.com/DS101** to help you on your way.

I hope you will join me on my daily broadcasts, so I can answer your questions and help you arrive safely at your ultimate destination. When you do, you will recognize the way I close every broadcast to keep you focused on the possibilities.

I want to remind you, like I always do, to...

Dream it,

Believe it,

Achieve it!

Vicki Fitch

Follow Us on Social Media!

Facebook @VickiFitch1   **Twitter @VickiFitch**

Instagram @Vicki_Fitch   **LinkedIn @VickiFitch**

Periscope @Vicki_Fitch   **Pinterest @VickiFitch**

PREFACE

I want to thank you for choosing this book. There are a lot of choices out there to teach you things, and I feel honored that you chose mine. With my more than thirty years of experience in business, I have invested in some great books and courses, as well as some that were a complete waste of my time and money. It is my sincere hope that you find this to be one of the most valuable resources in your business-building arsenal.

Although I have titled this book *Direct Selling 101* (*DS 101*), it goes far beyond the Direct Sales model. I have used examples from multiple industries and emphasized the core skills needed for the new entrepreneur as well as for someone who wants to be the executive of their own life. I originally wrote this book over fifteen years ago, but times have changed. While I was updating it to include modern day vernacular and incorporate information on **Social Media, Livestreaming,** and the internet, I realized there was so much content here; it could overwhelm a person who was just starting out.

For that reason, I separated the initial content into five separate books. *DS 101* provides a solid overview of Direct Sales, with an emphasis on the most important topics of how to Sell, Schedule, Recruit, Follow Up, and Overcome Objections. More importantly, it addresses how to face and overcome **FEAR** while finding your **Tribe** and gaining the support of your family and friends.

Besides just understanding how to build your business, you will enjoy building your character and **Confidence** while laughing at my mistakes and celebrating my victories. I've included step-by-step instructions, role playing conversations, anecdotes, and analogies that are sure to build on your natural talents.

This book is the perfect companion to any **New Consultant Training**, or to add foundational support to a seasoned pro. It is an easy read for your team members and it will free you up to focus on your industry specifics, while they start here, mastering the basics.

If you read the Introduction, you know this book is part of the **#12Books12Months** project. Below are the working titles of the upcoming Direct Sales series. It is possible that the titles have or will be changed or altered for clarity.

Direct Selling 201: Advanced Sales and Leadership Strategies to **#RockThatTeam** in Direct Sales and Beyond

Direct Selling 301: The Entrepreneur's Guide to Using Social Media & Live Video to **#RockThatStream** in Direct Sales and Beyond

Direct Selling 401: Marketing the True You to Build Your Brand to **#RockThatScene** in Direct Sales and Beyond.

Direct Selling 501: The Entrepreneur's Guide to Making Big Money to **#RockThatMachine** with Automation, Affiliation & Offloading in Direct Sales and Beyond

These volumes include a deep dive into Sales, Recruiting, Leadership, Networking, **Social Media**, and more topics that will help you grow as a person and an entrepreneur. I have made notations throughout the book to assist you in identifying which upcoming titles would provide more detailed information on specific topics. However, I recommend you read the books in the order they come out because each one really does build on the others.

If you have been following my **Livestreaming** or are part of my **Entrepreneurial Rock Stars** community, you probably already know my story and therefore, can skip the next paragraph. However, for those of you who don't, I would like to introduce myself.

I am a Direct Sales **Expert**. I've spent more than twenty years in the industry, placing Top 10 Internationally in Sales and Recruiting for more than a decade. No matter what business you are in, getting to the Top 10 is tricky. Staying there for ten years takes consistent effort and a commitment to growing and learning as a leader, an entrepreneur, and an individual. In addition to that, I built and sold four successful companies in various industries. So, I know what it is like to be a solopreneur as well as a corporation, hiring, training, scheduling, and educating staff and clients.

I became a master at **Systems** and **Procedures**, which has allowed me to balance my own schedule with multiple companies while having family members with ADHD, Asperger's, and learning disabilities. In addition, there was **Alcoholism** & **Addiction** in my extended family, which made for some interesting stories I will share with you throughout the year.

I **Believe** having transparency about my own circumstances shows that I can relate to you and your challenges. At some point, it is likely that I felt the same way you do now, or the way you will feel in the future. Whether you are feeling elated and excited, discouraged and disappointed, or overwhelmed and exhausted… I have been there too. And I survived.

I have a saying:

"Mentors are like bumper guards at the bowling alley… there is no reason for you to end up in the gutter."

I want to be your mentor, so I can decrease your learning curve, which will increase your **Productivity** and thus your profits. I know you may want to blaze your own trail, but I recommend you do that after you have become an **Expert**. Once you have mastered the skills in this series, you may find yourself writing a book like this from the top of #**RockThatDream** Ridge. (Be sure to send me a copy!)

You learn a lot about someone when you take a trip with them and this **#12Books12Months** journey is going to reveal a lot about me. The main thing I want you to know, is that I really do care. I don't have to know you personally to have a heart for you and your **Dreams**. I want to see you living them in a balanced and healthy way. (Yes! I do **Believe** it is possible.)

My prayer is that this book will touch the lives of those who need it and inspire everyone to become the best version of themselves.

So again, thank you for allowing me into this part of your life. I hope you find me an entertaining and educational companion.

Now, let's get to work!

Chapter 1

WHAT IS DIRECT SALES?

*"Most people are skeptical of what I do because society
has taught us to look for jobs, not opportunity."*
– Unknown

There is a lot of confusion about what **Direct Sales** is, and how it compares to **Multi-Level Marketing** or **Network Marketing**. There is even confusion from people who are already in the industry, so I am going to break it down from my perspective. Although all three terms are often, correctly, interchanged for one another, I want to clarify a few things.

NOTE: Each organization has different titles for their independent sales force. For the most part, I will be referring to them as Consultants or Representatives. There are also different names for the people who bring someone into the organization. I will use the term Upline to represent the person who recruits and Downline to represent the person or people who are recruited.

What They Have in Common

Before breaking down how they may be considered different, it is important to understand how they are the same.

1. These organizations are built with an independent sales force. They have a corporate infrastructure, but the representatives are not employees. They are independent business owners that agree to a set of conditions outlined by the company they chose to represent.

2. Each type of organization rewards their consultants in one or more of the following ways:
   - Earning commission on their personal sales.
   - Earning commission from the production of their **Downline**. (Each company calculates this differently. It will be outlined in their agreement.)
   - Earning bonuses based on selling, recruiting, or achieving specific requirements or titles.
   - Earning residual income based on monthly, recurring, or membership sales.
   - Earning incentives, car allowances, gifts, and trips.

3. These organizations don't typically spend much money on advertising. They depend on word-of-mouth advertising from their consultants.

Understanding the Origins

Direct Sales (DS) is typically a direct-to-consumer sale, where a representative either purchases wholesale from the company and resells it at a profit to the consumer or the consumer purchases retail from the website. The representatives are then paid their commissions on a daily, weekly, or monthly basis. This is also referred to as the "**Party Plan**" industry because these companies usually introduce their products to the marketplace by having some type of party or event. Inventory is sometimes recommended, but not usually necessary to have.

Style: Although a lot of this is done online, face-to-face events are still part of their success model.

Explanation: Companies like Mary Kay, Avon, and the original Creative Memories are part of the DS model. Many earlier companies like Avon started with a single level compensation plan, but later adjusted to a **Multi-Level Marketing** plan.

*NOTE: During my tenure with Creative Memories, they made a specific distinction. They were a **Direct Sales** company with 3-Tiers of Compensation. They did not refer to themselves as an **MLM**. The focus was building relationships with customers and recruiting people who wanted to operate a business.*

Multi-Level Marketing (MLM) refers to the compensation structure
paid by the company to their representatives. As the name suggests, instead of paying a single level of compensation, this plan pays on multiple levels. This practice encouraged **Uplines** to actively participate in training and supporting additional team members.

Style: Much of the **MLM** model is now done online.

Explanation: Although MLM originally started as a reference to the way the representatives were paid, another distinction arose. The MLM companies chose to focus on recruiting representatives to purchase their own products at wholesale and find others to do the same instead of finding individuals who wanted to sell to others at retail. Amway is one of the original MLM companies.

Network Marketing (NM) refers to a business where a network of other
distributors is needed for the business to grow.

Explanation: The name Network Marketing was often used as a substitute for **Multi-Level Marketing** when **MLMs** were being scrutinized due to the **Pyramid Scheme** craze and some overzealous marketing in the industry. The companies focused on **MLM/Network Marketing** often have significantly higher bonus compensation opportunities for the **Upline** leaders than the part of the industry focused on **Direct Sales**.

As a whole, the industry is continually evolving with new options and opportunities. Looking at their 130-year history, Avon is a great example. Their door-to-door "Avon Calling" campaigns gave birth to the **Party Plan** industry, which morphed into on-line sales and events as technology emerged. The original one-on-one model grew to heights that weren't previously imagined. (check out the original "Ding Dong, Avon Calling" video at **www.VickiFitch.com/DS101)**

Single tiers of compensation grew to multiple tiers and car bonuses turned into million-dollar opportunities to entice more people to get involved with the industry. Companies are changing with the times and are now blending styles and compensation packages. They are trying to create the most lucrative option, so they can attract the best representatives, whom they are willing to reward generously. These **Hybrid** companies are the next generation of the industry.

Hybrid

Hybrid is what I call a company that combines the different styles of the industry. It may involve **Direct Sales** to the consumer, a **Multi-Level Marketing** compensation package, and often a recurring membership or subscription model which can produce residual income for as long as you are a representative of the company.

Explanation: LegalShield is a great example of a **Hybrid** company. They engage in the Direct Sales model of direct-to-consumer sales and incorporate B2B (Business to Business). They utilize the **Multi-Level Marketing** compensation structure. They have a subscription-based service that provides residual income for the duration of their involvement with the company, as well as large bonuses for achieving specific goals that draw in serious entrepreneurs.

Oftentimes, **MLM** companies are referred to or considered as **Pyramid Schemes**. Let me explain what that means and differentiate the two.

Pyramid Scheme

Pyramid Scheme is an "investment" where each participant recruits two additional people to invest. The enticement for getting involved, is the possibility of receiving a big payout, based on the people who "invest" after them.

Explanation: Wikipedia states that there are **Pyramids** posing as **MLM** companies. This can happen when the company pays the representatives specifically to recruit other people. A portion of the "initiation fee" is usually what is given to the recruiter. Often, in these situations, there are no products or services; it is simply a distribution of the participants' initiation fees.

Personal Experience

I am embarrassed to say that I can speak about this from personal experience. When I was eighteen, I accidentally got involved with an actual **Pyramid Scheme**. My first clue should have been that there were literally pyramids drawn on boards around the room. In my own defense, **Pyramid Schemes** weren't widely known about, or warned against, at the time.

The way the pyramid is structured, you come in on the bottom with $1,000 per person. Each time someone new comes in, you get pushed up the pyramid. When you get to the top spot, you get $10,000. If you got in at the very beginning, you would make it to the top because there were a lot of other suckers coming in behind you. There were weekly meetings with all the pyramid standings for you to see how you were climbing the ladder. It is a bit comical as I look back on it now. Susceptibility has a lot to do with trusting the other people who invited you to participate.

If you were one of the unlucky ones like me, in any of the last nine spots, you got zilch, zip, nada, nothing. I wasn't very happy with the "friends" who encouraged me to do this. They prodded me to invest, while reminding me they had already "cashed out" twice and reinvested.

The idea behind perpetuating the pyramid was that each person would bring in two friends. Theoretically, the pyramid should go on forever, but it doesn't, and it won't. I didn't invite my friends to join me on this venture. I was willing to take a gamble on my money because of the success my friends shared. I was **not** willing to gamble my reputation.

My reason for sharing my mishap with you is for you to know that I understand the concern and reluctance of people who are worried that this industry might operate like that.

Keep this in mind: If no product or service is being sold, and people are being paid solely based on the people they bring in to the organization, that is a **Pyramid Scheme** structure.

If someone must "lose", I don't recommend you play.

Without a product or service, eventually, the line will end, and someone will be left empty-handed. If someone must "lose", I don't recommend you play.

A lesson learned the hard way is still extremely valuable. All education comes at a cost; just make sure you are willing to pay the price or find another form of education. I always say,

---

"The School of Hard Knocks... is an EXCELLENT educator."

Learn from your experiences and use them to make better decisions in the future. Do not let a previous "education" stop you from pursuing your **Dreams** with a quality company that offers value to you, your customers, and your community.

It's time to raise your sails, as we set off for **Success Island**. While we are sailing across the seas, I'd love to share my entrepreneurial journey with you.

It started when I was twelve...

Chapter 2

MY STORY

*"If it's important to you, you will find
a way. If not, you will find an excuse."*
– Ryan Blair

When I was twelve years old, I wanted a phone line in my room. For those of you who are Millennials, Gen Z or beyond, we didn't get an iPhone when we were six years old. Back then, it was a curly corded phone attached to a wall. The entire family (or the entire world, depending on whether the doors were open) got to participate in your phone call. Not the ideal situation for a burgeoning pre-teen.

My father was a twenty-one-year veteran in the Navy who retired as a Chief. He then started his own trucking business here in California. He believed in the power of hard work, dedication, and commitment to excellence. These were traits I admired in him, until I asked if I could get a phone line in my room. His answer was clear, "I am NOT paying for you to get a phone line in your room. You will have to pay for it yourself."

I can tell you that as disappointed as I was, I definitely saw this as a "win". If you are wondering why I would consider that a win, it is because this was one of the only times in my life when the answer wasn't "No." He gave me **Hope**, and that is a powerful thing!

Simply put, if I could come up with the money, I could have what I wanted. If you know anything about me, you know that I am one determined girl! The wheels started churning, but they didn't need to go far. A friend of my father's was there that day, and he owned an insurance agency. Like most small businesses, he needed leads. He agreed to pay me for each person who allowed him to provide them an insurance quote.

You may be wondering why anyone would consider letting a twelve-year-old girl represent them in any professional capacity. Well, I admit, I am a bit of an enigma. Instead of playing with dolls, I spent most of my time talking to adults. I would sit and listen to my parents' conversations and paid attention to their word choices. I became a virtual sponge, processing all the information I could. I learned to think before I spoke and developed a very mature demeanor. I was a very confident person with an extensive vocabulary. I was also a very quick thinker.

Talking on the phone would be simple. I knew how to ask good questions and how to wait for the answers...

"When can I start?" I asked as I sat there staring at him, waiting for his answer.

He chuckled for a second before he caught himself and said, "How about now?"

I recognized it was possible he just wanted to get rid of me, so they could go back to playing cribbage, but I didn't care. I was ready for the challenge and I was ready for a phone! Nothing was getting in the way of my success. That curly corded beauty was going to be mine!

I was a trusting young soul and I didn't even ask how much he would pay me. I went to the china cabinet and grabbed the phone book. (Yes, there was no internet back then and we actually had to look people's numbers up in the white pages!) I proceeded to my parent's bedroom, where the only other phone in the house was located. I opened the phonebook to begin my quest.

My conversations went something like this.

Me: "Hello? May I speak to Aaron, please?"

Aaron: "This is Aaron."

Me: "Hi Aaron, my name is Vicki with Farmers Insurance and I was just calling today to see if you would be interested in getting a free quote on your insurance?"

Aaron: "Hmm… I suppose it can't hurt to get a free quote."

Me: "Great! I will have Mr. Brunner call you tomorrow at this number. Is this same time OK?"

Come to think of it, I may have been one of the original Telemarketers… before they were considered "not cool."

I went through the list for about forty minutes and came out with approximately twenty-six names of people who were ready for appointments. Fred's mouth dropped open and his eyes went wide in surprise. Looking back, I'm not sure if it was from sheer joy or because he didn't actually expect me to do it.

Either way, my entrepreneurial spark was ignited, and the fire only burned brighter from there. At the time, I didn't realize how this skill was going to support every other business I started. I was willing to work for what I wanted, and I realized that people would PAY me to SOLVE their problems! This opened my eyes to a new way of thinking, which is what drove me to becoming a successful **Serial Entrepreneur**.

Needless to say, I had just been hired for my first job, and I was proud! The next day, my father called and scheduled the installation of the phone line. He loaned me the money for the installation and the first month's bill. I'd like to say that my Dad did that because he was so proud of me (which I know he was), but I think it was more likely that he wanted his phone back since I was making calls for three hours a day!

I continued to work every evening, making calls after school. I was committed to my responsibility to pay my father back, and to making my employer proud.

Now that I had the "business bug", I found a lot of new ways to solve people's problems (**Pain Points**), which led me to numerous entrepreneurial endeavors as a teenager. I will save those stories for another book; knowing that, lays the foundation for the next part of my story.

Fast forward to seven years later, at the age of nineteen, I bought my first house here in California.

Dream and Believe

If you know the cost of homes in California, you know this is no small feat! My first hurdle was finding people to take my search seriously. Most teenagers aren't purchasing real estate, so it requires **Confidence** in yourself to seek out people who are willing to help. It also requires a focused commitment to save the money needed for the down payment and to have the reserves the bank needs for them to consider you a good financial risk.

When I originally told people, I was going to buy a house, I was excited by my choice and I thought my friends would be, too. I wasn't expecting a barrage of **FEAR** to be unleashed on my **Dream**. I share this with you, not to discourage you, but to prepare you. When you aren't prepared, the stampede of **Doubt** can trample your **Confidence** and leave you feeling overwhelmed.

Instead of "Wow, that's fantastic!" or "Congratulations!"

I heard, "Wow, are you crazy?" "That is too much responsibility." and "You're too young."

I am bringing this up because you are going to face some opposition, too. The **Naysayers**, for whatever reason, will try to discourage you from reaching beyond the **Sea of Sameness** they are swimming in. The important thing is to keep believing in yourself. I chose to **Believe** that they meant well, but the **Bully** in my head proved to be a mighty adversary. (I have written an entire book called *Evict the Bully in Your Head* to help you combat this foe and send him packing.)

Where **Confidence** stood only moments before, **Doubt** had now stepped in. The thoughts ringing in my head…

"What if they are right?"

"What if I can't afford it?"

"What if I make a mistake?"

It takes time to recover from **Doubt,** but **Confidence** reminded me to use logic.

- I had a realtor who believed in me and spent her time showing me properties.
- I had a bank willing to loan me the money.
- I had a seller who chose me out of the various bids she received.
- I had a sister willing to partner with me.

Making the choice to **Believe** in yourself when those you are close to think you are foolish is a difficult thing. It felt good and satisfying to make the decision, but it also felt scary. I recognized that if I was wrong, I might find myself alone.

Now imagine that six months later, you tell those same people you have decided to quit your job and start a bookkeeping and tax company.

The surprised faces, shaking heads, and rolling eyes prompted the same series of questions.

"Are you crazy?"

"You just bought a house and that is too much responsibility."

"You're too young; people will never take you seriously."

"You could ruin your credit."

FEAR and **Anxiety** started haunting me.

"What if they are right and this is the wrong move?"

"What if no one will take me seriously?"

"What if I lose the house and ruin my credit?"

This time, I was a little more prepared since I had already gone through this. I had to remind myself.

"I'm NOT Crazy. If I make the wrong move, I will adjust my course and recover."

Logic says that if an entrepreneur hired the twelve-year-old version of me to book appointments, the more experienced version of me has a lot more to offer. After all, my dad trusted me to do his books when I was thirteen. Other business owners will trust me to take care of theirs now that I'm twenty.

I had to ask myself, "What is the worst thing that could happen? I'm not going to die."

I know that to some of you, not accomplishing a goal you set out to do would feel like a pain worse than death. If you are thinking, "That is easy for you to say, Vicki.", think again. I grew up in a military household where the kitchen wasn't clean unless the faucet was shining. (No, I am not kidding.)

I believed **Perfection** was what my parents were looking for and although I always fell short, I unrealistically started to expect it of myself. I call that the "**Pain of Perfectionism**". It is a wound that is much deeper than most people recognize, but I lived with that nagging feeling that I was never enough…

That feeling tried to hold me captive and convince me to stay stuck in the **Sea of Mediocrity,** but I refused to let it. I wanted to grow and mature and I knew that sometimes meant taking calculated and educated risks. The truth was I did **Believe** in myself, but I was letting the concern of others challenge my resolve.

That is when I came up with this quote:

"Don't tell me I can't do it, until I've already done it… then feel free to let me know!"

To make a long story short, yes, I quit my job, started my own company, and became one of the top franchises in the country. I was written up in a magazine and became a very notable and respected member of my community. My risk paid off and my **Confidence** in my decision-making abilities grew.

New Adventures

After about five years, I sold that company to take a position to help my fiancée. Terry was the Vice President of a publicly traded company and he wanted me to build up a division that was not living up to its potential. I excelled at that, quadrupling the revenue in less than a year.

When we got married, we both left our six-figure jobs and started a construction company. Terry had his C-53 Contractors License, and we had noticed a **Pain Point** in the industry we knew we could solve. Within three months of starting the company from scratch, we were already profitable, and it continued to grow. This is where things got tricky.

We both wanted a family and agreed that when I got pregnant, I would retire to be a stay-at-home mom. I was committed to making sure my family was well taken care of. When I got pregnant, I hired someone to take over running the office for me. The only problem was the business was still growing so fast that by the time I had my replacement trained, we needed another staff member just to keep up with the growing needs of the company. It took me a few years to finally get out, but during my pregnancy, I was introduced to Scrapbooking!

Many of you may not know this about me, but I LOVE SCRAPBOOKING! Now I had no idea how to do it "right" when I started. I just put construction paper, cards, and miscellaneous stuff in those old peel and stick albums and was proud of my creations. During my pregnancy, I was introduced to Creative Memories... and I was hooked! The hormones, history, and my love of crafty things, created the perfect storm of a new hobby that HAD to be in my life.

I was going to make the "Perfect" scrapbooks for my baby. That **Pain of Perfectionism** reared its ugly head again, which I will discuss in more depth in future books in this series.

It's All About the Questions

I started scrapbooking and fell in love with the papers, stickers, die-cuts, and fun. I never thought of it as a business, just as a wonderful hobby. I was a busy woman who didn't have time to mess around. When I had my scrapbooking time, I wanted to make sure I had everything I needed. My mantra with my consultant was, "Buy me 2 of EVERYTHING New."

This is a true story. What Direct Sales person doesn't want a customer like that? Seriously, we ARE out there. You just need the **Courage** to understand that and help solve our **Pain Point**. (More details about that in **Chapter 12: How to be A Stellar Seller**).

I was the perfect customer with a credit card on file and a steady stream of products every month. I was happy as could be until one day, she asked me if I had ever thought of being a consultant...

In my head, I was saying…

"Me? Are you crazy? I've got a company that is growing so fast I can't get out, and a newborn I am dying to spend more time with. I only have time for this when he is napping."

Verbally, I said, "No, I'm too busy."

If you have already started your recruiting journey, you will recognize that this is a very common objection. In **Chapter 14: Rock Star Recruiting** I am going to give you the "Magic Formula" to get past that hurdle and enable you to recruit Top 10 Stellar Sellers like me! Keep on reading!

Back to my conversation… She accepted my answer, placed my order, and we both went on our merry way. Several weeks later, I needed something else and called to place another order. When she called me back with the total, she did something very smart… take notes here!

She said, "Vicki, I just wanted you to know how much you would have saved if you were a consultant." But, she didn't stop there… she continued with,

"I actually added up what you would have saved on all your purchases."

When she told me how much, I was shocked. No matter how financially stable you are, finding out you could have saved that much money is a bit sobering! And what was my answer?

"Let me talk to my husband."

Have you ever heard that one? Let's look at this situation with honesty and clarity for a moment.

I didn't *need* to talk to my husband. The cost of the kit was less than what I was spending on products. It wasn't a financial decision, nor was it about me asking him about spending the money. Like most decisions, I needed more information to be sure I wasn't getting into something like a **Pyramid Scheme** (LOL). If she asked me the RIGHT questions and had been prepared to overcome a few standard objections, I would probably have signed up right then.

I asked her a few more questions and told her I would get back to her after I spoke to him. He is a businessman and when I told him how much I would have saved, his answer was,

"Why haven't you done it already?"

It truly was a **no-brainer**, and I signed up immediately. I still didn't see this as a business. I saw it more as a permanent 30% off coupon that included over $500 worth of products for $199.

It wasn't until later that I recognized what a lucrative opportunity it was, and that it would allow me the **F**reedom and **F**lexibility to work around my **F**amily's schedule. Those were a lot of "F" words, so it makes perfect sense to talk about some more…

Chapter 3

THE "F" WORDS

"If it doesn't challenge you, it won't change you."
– Fred DeVito

'm a Christian woman, and as a matter of respect to my Lord and my family, I have a very G-Rated vocabulary. I don't judge other people who choose the colorful side of language, but I do share a tip with them.

"No one loses a job because they DON'T swear, but they could lose one, because they DO."

That being said, it is common to think that when people talk about the "F" Word or "4-Letter Words", they are referencing a subset of words that I would typically consider to be outside of the G-Rating vocabulary I use. I want to first talk about a couple words that combine both of those distinctions. In my opinion, these "4-Letter "F" Words" can be doubly damaging. They do much of their damage on the inside by discouraging you and your precious **Dreams**. They can affect the core of who you are and what you will become. I want you to know what they are, so you can eliminate them, or at least use them sparingly, especially as they apply to yourself.

Our First "F" Word—FAIL

In my world, FAIL is a 4-Letter "F" Word.

In my world, FAIL is a 4-Letter "F" Word.

I don't **Believe** we ever FAIL. I know that is a strong statement, but I truly **Believe** that the things that didn't go the way we planned are **Stepping Stones**. They are a reminder that there is another way to accomplish the task or to solve the problem. Giving up should not be an option for an entrepreneur. We must persevere.

The only real FAILURE is the refusal to try.

When we learn something new, it is rarely done the best it can be done on our first try. We learn from trying things repeatedly, adjusting as necessary. That is the same way inventions are improved and eventually perfected.

Let's look at this definition of the word Fail from Dictionary.com to gain some perspective.

Fail [feyl]—to break, bend, crush, or be otherwise destroyed or made *useless* because of an excessive load.

Think about the weight of that word and its meaning. Most of the time, we choose to discard things that are referred to as broken, bent, crushed, destroyed, or useless.

Dr. Spencer Silver is famous for trying to create an incredibly strong adhesive for the aerospace industry. Unfortunately, his efforts created the exact opposite of his goal. He developed one of the weakest adhesives available.

Creating something that is the opposite of your objective would be considered a FAILURE in most cases, because it would be deemed *useless* for its intended purpose.

There are three ways to view this setback:

1. Failure—Completely missed the mark and the work should be disposed of.

2. **Stepping Stone**—We learn something from the process and choose to amplify what worked and replace what didn't.

3. Find an alternative use—Celebrate the properties of what we have made and find a **Pain Point** that can be solved with the new creation.

In this case, Dr. Silver chose Option 2 and 3. He recognized what he needed to improve for the original project **and** thought of additional ways to use the substance that he accidentally created. He faced a lot of challenges, setbacks, and rejections regarding the new product. But the end, he developed one of the most successful office supplies of all time... The Post-it Note.

What was literally useless for its intended purpose became the solution to a myriad of **Pain Points.** He made history with what some would have called a complete and utter FAILURE.

The truth is, both you and your ideas are valuable. You do not FAIL when you set out to do something but do not achieve it. **Reframe** the situation and recognize all your efforts are part of your entrepreneurial education. Removing that 4-Letter "F" Word and replacing it with something more accurate will keep your vision clear and your emotions positive. Challenges happen all the time, recognize they are set backs and use them as **Stepping Stones** to propel you on to something amazing like Dr. Silver did.

While we are talking about 4-Letter "F" Words, I think it is time we talk about the big kahuna, **FEAR**.

Our Second "F" Word—FEAR

I don't want to spoil *Evict the Bully in Your Head* for you, but I will tell you that **FEAR** is one of the leading characters. It is imperative you understand this adversary and his minions. The weight of these villains can strangle you and suffocate your **Dreams.**

People **FEAR** a wide variety of things but a few that tend to plague entrepreneurs are:

- **FEAR** of FAILURE
- **FEAR** of Judgement
- **FEAR** of Ridicule
- **FEAR** of the Unknown
- **FEAR** of Success

FEAR is a formidable foe, but he can be stopped when we choose to **Reframe** the situation.

We already addressed your **FEAR of FAILURE** by remembering to view our setbacks as **Stepping Stones** and by remembering Dr. Silver's example.

FEAR of Judgement—People who are floating in the **Ocean of Overwhelm** tend to concentrate on Judging others. They are usually insecure or unhappy with themselves or their accomplishments. When you keep that in mind, it's easier to understand that they are trying to deflect their own **FEAR** onto you to avoid looking at what they consider are their own shortcomings.

FEAR of Ridicule—Those who are stuck in the **Depths of Discouragement** use Ridicule as a lifeline to drag others down, so they are not alone. Similar to their neighbors in the **Ocean of Overwhelm**, these participants are insecure about who they are, what they look like, and their lack of abilities. They are often consumed with what others think of them and spend time trying to discourage other people from achieving their **Dreams**.

FEAR of the Unknown—Those stuck in the **Sea of Status Quo** don't have the **Courage** to **Believe** in themselves and move beyond the comfort of predictability. When nothing changes, they know what to expect and there is no chance of letting anyone down. This is where **Dreams** go to die.

FEAR of Success—The **Tide of Temptation** is holding these people hostage. They have accepted false truths and have been conditioned to **Believe** inaccurate information. They **FEAR** success may corrupt them or that their **Dreams** are too far out of reach. They are Tempted to **Believe** they could make it to shore, but each time they get near, **FEAR** convinces them it will just lead to disappointment. They allow the Tide to drag them back out to sea…over and over.

Recognizing that **FEAR** is trying to distract you from your **Dreams** is your first step to conquering and taking control of it. The second is to **Reframe** the situation to get an accurate perspective. And third, read *Evict the Bully in Your Head* so you fully understand why these **Bullies** have such a strong hold and how to start the eviction process.

Our next "F" Word—FILTER

In order to understand your **FILTER**, we must first understand your **Lens**.

Just as a camera needs a lens to capture images, your **Lens**, records your history. It is a compilation of your journey through life. In essence, it is your "reality".

Photographers often add a filter to protect the lens, or to distribute the light differently, to enhance their images. If the wrong filter is used, the image can be blurred or distorted.

Your experiences and your relationships create your **FILTERS**. Your self-esteem and the way others treat you, affect your clarity.

Insults and negativity are like mud on your **FILTER**; they can easily distort what you see even though the landscape hasn't changed. Having low self-esteem is like wiping the mud off with a dirty hand. Although the view is clearer, it is still obstructed with smudges and smears.

Compliments and encouragement are like windshield wiper fluid; they break down the grime to clear the **FILTER**. High self-esteem is like having automatic windshield wipers; they wipe away the negative influences as soon as they appear. The more positive your self-esteem, the cleaner your **FILTER** will be.

It is important to understand that when you experience extended periods of negativity, the composition of the debris changes from mud, which might simply blur or obstruct your **FILTER**, to rocks, which can cause it to pit, mar, or even crack. This is why it is imperative you choose to avoid these negative influences and immerse yourself in positive ones whenever possible.

Since we have been talking about cameras, let's add another term from the photographic world… FOCUS.

Our Fourth "F" Word is—FOCUS

There is a quote that says:

> *"What you THINK about, you BRING About." – Bob Proctor*

In other words, what you FOCUS on is what you will experience the most of. In my family, we like to play a game called "**Bright Side**!" It is a game where we specifically "Train our Brain" to focus on the **Bright Side** of things, searching for whatever positive we can find in a situation. The following is an example of how playing this game will not only affect you, but also the people who spend time with you.

Bright Side

One extremely rainy afternoon, my family and I were driving down the street. Dark clouds were everywhere, and the rain was coming down hard. Suddenly, my window slowly started rolling down and rain began pelting me in the face. Startled, and honestly a bit frustrated, I turned to my husband, perplexed at why he would roll my window down in the middle of a rainstorm.

At that moment, he turned to ask me the same question I was about to ask him. Seeing the shock on each other's faces, we realized that the power window on the van had gone out. As inconvenient as it was, our only option was to drive to the dealership to get it repaired.

Admittedly, I was feeling irritated as there was no way for me to get away from the rain that was now plastering my hair all over my face. In addition, I realized that I looked like someone who had just wet her pants as the rain had soaked my lap, given its unobstructed entrance into our vehicle. (Here is where my consistently being a positive influence, paid off.)

From his car seat in the back of the van, my son shouted,

"**BRIGHT SIDE**! You don't have to take a shower today!"

We all started laughing out loud. The mascara dripping down my face was now a part of a comedic family moment, instead of something that could have ruined our entire day. That kind of change of FOCUS is powerful and has lasting impact.

The moral of that story is to seek the **#BrightSide** in all situations. It will help you create the stability you need for our next "F" word FOUNDATION.

Our Fifth "F" Word— FOUNDATION

I **Believe** that to run a successful business, you need to have a firm FOUNDATION, which includes the principles to guide your business growth.

Since you are reading this book, I have to assume that you actually WANT to make money in this industry. I imagine that living a life of financial freedom, while doing something you enjoy, is what you secretly hope for (even if you aren't willing to admit it out loud.) Since you took the time to start reading this book, then you WANT to **Believe** it is possible and I'm here to help you navigate your way to **Success Island.**

Know your WHAT before your WHY

When we are in school, no one teaches us to **Dream.** When you are in high school trying to figure out a future career path, no one asks,

"What do you LOVE to do?"

Our inspiration for making a lifelong career choice is usually based on a family business, a direction our parents want us to take, an opportunity someone shares with us, or the allure of a high paying job.

We may also have been swayed by school testing results that highlighted what career our aptitude suggests is best suited for us. I am a firm believer in looking for something you LOVE to do and learning how to monetize it. In the Direct Sales Industry, there are extensive choices available to match with your interests.

The criteria we use to choose a Direct Sales company is similar.

- We hear a lot of hype about a company and catch the **FOMO (Fear of Missing Out).**
- A friend joins the company and they convince us to come along for the ride.

- We hear that there is a LOT of money to be made and all we have to do is "sign on the dotted line."
- We resonate with a leader or a company's mission that is near and dear to our hearts.
- We want to get our own products at a discount.

All of these reasons have merit. They contribute to fun, excitement, engagement, relationships, finances, etc. However, the real question you should be asking yourself is,

"What do you LOVE to do?"

If you really want to make money in Direct Sales, you need to know WHAT you want to do before we focus on WHY you want to do it.

Many sales professionals want you to focus on your WHY. I agree that your WHY keeps you grounded, focused, and steady during challenging times. On the bad days (and there will be some), you need to fall back on your WHY to keep you moving forward. However, you must remember that your WHY is lacking a strong FOUNDATION if you don't LOVE what you are doing.

Be honest with yourself... Do you LOVE what you do?

Do you LOVE what you do?

If not, is it because times are tough and the glamour has worn off, or your original reason for starting no longer inspires you? Sometimes, we long to do something different because the flame that once burned bright is being doused by **Doubt** or **FEAR**.

By the time you finish these books, you will not only recognize what drives your feelings, but you will have a much better grasp on how to use them to serve you. For that reason, I encourage you to finish the **#12Books12Months** series before making any changes. All the skills you learn will serve you in any industry, but understanding yourself, will give you better clarity to truly *#RockThatDream*.

It is my goal to help you achieve not only financial prosperity, but to also to help you experience those all-expense paid incentive trips and find true and lasting friendships. Add those things together with doing something you LOVE while having the freedom of working your own schedule, and you will understand what success really is.

Now you know what creates a solid FOUNDATION. Next, we need to add in the perfect blend of **Planning** and preparation.

Chapter 4

PLANNING AND PREPARATION

"Planning without action is futile. Action without planning is fatal."
– Cornelius Fichtner

It has been my experience that new entrepreneurs tend to think that starting a business is a 24/7 commitment. There is nothing that will produce burnout faster than running yourself ragged and not having a plan to keep your life in balance. It is essential that you make some decisions on what you want and what you are willing to give, in order to get it.

When you make the decision to start a business, you must choose how many hours a week or a month you are willing to put in. I realize some of you will say, "As many as it takes!", but that answer is too broad and lacks the depth to create an execution strategy.

Committing to goals and objectives requires you to take an actual look at your life and your schedule, before you can decide how many hours you have available to invest in your endeavor. Then, it is critical that you figure out how to maximize the value of your time on **income producing** activities.

Just for clarification purposes, filing paperwork and reorganizing inventory to avoid making phone calls are NOT income-producing activities. They are important parts of your business, but you must prioritize things that will generate income, so you can be profitable.

It's All in the Planning

You would probably agree there aren't many people in the world today who are running around saying, "I've got an extra twenty to thirty hours a week, and I was hoping you could help me fill them!"

I am going to assume for the moment that you are a busy person and that adding on something new to your schedule will take some focus and coordination. If I am wrong, kudos to you! I celebrate your success in this area. If your life is a well-oiled machine, I'm certain that you understand the art of **Planning** ahead, and you recognize the value of Time Management.

"Time Management is the skill you most urgently need to master."

I have seen more people abandon their entrepreneurial pursuits because they lack the skills to manage their time, than people who no longer wanted to participate in their industry. Since one of the greatest hurdles to effectively running your own business is time management, I created a course to help entrepreneurs excel in this area.

The Rock Star Guide to Gettin' It Done

As a serial entrepreneur, I am often asked how I can operate multiple businesses and manage my household without cloning myself.

Over the last 30 years, I developed a system for handling all the different responsibilities of being a wife, mother, daughter, friend, volunteer, leader, coach, author, speaker, **Livestreamer**, podcaster, and entrepreneur. **The Rock Star Guide to Gettin' It Done (RSG2GID)** is a Step-by-Step Organization and Execution System designed to help people get MORE done in LESS time. The tagline is, "It will change your life… if you let it!"

Understanding all your responsibilities and how to fit them in as efficiently as possible, can be a difficult task. For some, it can seem impossible. It requires you to understand how to balance your energy and time blocks accordingly.

I want to encourage you, by letting you know, this system works. Imagine having extra time each week to do more of what you enjoy. Whether it is spending time with friends, working to build your business, or taking a vacation. Being in control of your schedule is the first step to being in control of your life.

If you have ever felt overwhelmed by the number of projects, tasks or responsibilities you have, you **need** this course. You will go through the exercises of identifying all the "Hats you Wear" and all the responsibilities that go along with each of them. I walk you through, step-by-step, in video format, identifying what your tasks are, prioritizing them, and creating a schedule that works for you and your active lifestyle.

I've even broken down my own schedule for you to see and provided all the resources for you to get started… TODAY. All the details can be found on the resource page **www.VickiFitch.com/DS101**. I highly recommend you get it and implement it as quickly as possible, so you can start experiencing the benefits.

For now, I want to highlight two activities from that course that will immediately improve your **Productivity**. Let me introduce you to the **Time Saving Twins—Group Tasking** and **Layering**.

Group Tasking

Group Tasking is when you combine things of a similar nature to do them all together. I call it the Peanut Butter & Jelly Theory.

The Peanut Butter & Jelly Theory of Time Management

If you are going to make ten Peanut Butter & Jelly sandwiches (PB & J's), which method do you think would be faster?

Method 1—Individual Sandwiches

- Pull out two pieces of bread
- Put PB on one side
- Put Jelly on the other
- Put the two pieces together

- Cut the sandwich
- Pull out two more pieces of bread
- Repeat until they are done

Method 2—Group Tasking

- Take out twenty pieces of bread
- Put PB on ten
- Put Jelly on ten
- Put all ten together
- Cut all ten sandwiches at once

Method 2—Group Tasking will save a tremendous amount of time. It is an easily provable theory. If you are questioning its validity, try the experiment and time yourself.

You should note that the activity wasn't done with less care, it was simply done faster and more efficiently. The more you implement **Group Tasking**, the more time you will have to do other things.

Layering

Layering is another way to save time. Please understand that it is NOT multi-tasking.

There are certain activities we do each day that do not require the active part of our brain. Walking, for instance, becomes something we can do in "**Auto Pilot**", meaning we can easily do another activity like listening to music at the same time.

"Layering is the process of engaging in multiple activities simultaneously without diluting your efficiency in any of them."

The key to **Layering** is for you to only perform one function that requires the active part of the brain while engaging in other **Auto Pilot** activities.

Example: Walking on the treadmill and listening to an audio book on personal development.

Walking on the treadmill does not require active participation of your brain, so listening to audio books, podcasts, or other material provides you with both the benefits of exercise and developing your expertise. It does not compromise the effectiveness of either activity.

Multi-Tasking is the attempt to engage in more than one activity, which requires the active part of your brain, at one time.

Example: Trying to talk on the phone and entering data into a spreadsheet. Some of you may feel you do this very well, but a high percentage of errors are recorded during times that multi-tasking is attempted.

When you start being proactive about **Group Tasking** and **Layering**, your **Productivity** will increase exponentially. If you are interested in getting more information for yourself and/or your team, go to **www.VickiFitch.com/DS101**. We can even provide bulk pricing and virtual or in-house training.

After you identify the activities you can use **Group Tasking** and **Layering** to accomplish, your next step is to create a schedule that includes them. The **RSG2GID** breaks this process into simple steps so you can figure out your **Non-Negotiables** while making time for your business.

Planning

Another critical part of success is **Planning** and creating appropriate time blocks for all the essential activities.

Of course, we need to schedule time to Sell, Schedule, and Recruit, but there are also things like paperwork, placing orders, filing and bookkeeping that must be done as well. In addition, you don't want to forget Customer Service, Follow Up, Marketing, Branding, and Leadership. Effectively maintaining these activities will decide if your business will either sizzle or fizzle.

Expectations

One of the reasons that there is so much attrition in this industry is because of unrealistic expectations. Representatives seem to think, (and this could be you too, so let me help set the record straight right now) when you join a Direct Sales company, all your friends and family should flock to your side to support you and purchase your new product or service.

I mean, that's what friends are for, right?

WRONG.

Although you may be one of the people who truly experience the strength of a family who participates in your events and invites their friends, this is actually more of a rare occurrence. Family and friends, although they often want to be supportive, will often start asking questions like,

"When are you going to get a real job?"

"Have you made a lot of money yet?" or

"Why do you bother when so few people show up?"

NOTE: The good news is, if you follow this series, you won't have to worry about any of those questions, because your success will be noticed.

Most of the time, their comments aren't designed to hurt you. Since they are not sensitive to how vulnerable it is to be an entrepreneur, they don't realize those comments are like little knives carving away your self-confidence. If your love of your business isn't strong enough, the moment you hit some hurdles, your first inclination will be to use their skepticism as your excuse for quitting.

Believing in yourself is hard work. When the world keeps telling you it isn't worth it, after a while it is easier to **Believe** them and join in the rhetoric than it is to stand up, dig in, and figure out how to do it better. When you allow your exposed feelings to influence your decisions, quitting seems easier than facing your feelings of "failure". When discouragement takes over, it is easy to just start agreeing with statements such as,

"You can't make money in this industry."

"The market is saturated." or

"There is too much competition."

Just to make sure I am crystal clear on this… those are all EXCUSES. **Yes, Excuses**, and if you ever want your **Dreams** to come true, you need to abandon excuses all together. In a book called *The Magic of Thinking Big* by David J. Schwartz, one of the chapters is called **Excusitis, the Failure Disease**. I wrote this book to help you build your business and to cure you of Excusitis. And sometimes, that is delivered with a simple **#Fitchslap**

What is a **Fitchslap**?

The Fitchslap is a public service.
It only comes out when necessary.
It is always done in Love,
and it is used to redirect the course
of someone who has gone astray.

If you find yourself making excuses for the progress you are making or not making, you have my permission to give yourself a mental **Fitchslap**. If you need one-on-one help with this, I do private and group coaching and would be happy to assist you and any of your teammates who need this gentle **Nudge** to get you back on track.

Ask yourself this… "Has anyone EVER made it in this industry?"

The answer is "YES!"

Many people have made it, so you don't even have to blaze the trail yourself. You just need to follow the leaders who have made it before you. When you are confident in your skill set, you can start blazing some new trails. It all starts with your WHAT, followed by your WHY. It also requires your **CONFIDENCE**.

"When you don't Believe in you, others will follow your lead."

The next step in being prepared is to become accountable to someone else. This should be someone who will care about your challenges and help you come up with creative ways around them. A person who encourages you and who believes in you, even when you **Doubt** yourself.

For some of you, your accountability partner may be your spouse or a friend. I must mention that a spouse is typically not the right person, because it is too easy to manipulate that relationship. When a significant other, tries to hold you accountable to your commitments, we all know that an argument might ensue. These disagreements will give you more reasons to make excuses.

One of my top tips for anyone who is serious about this industry is…

Hire a Business Coach

I'm not talking to those of you who just want to earn a little extra income on the side or are looking for a social outlet. I am talking to those of you who want to earn big money and want an experienced guide leading you to **#RockThatDream Ridge**.

Does it cost money? Yes, it does. It is an investment in yourself. Just like going to college costs money, think of it as you going to business school and getting your degree in Direct Sales. There is unlimited earning potential for people with **Drive** and **Determination;** no other skill is a pre-requisite. The rest can be learned.

No matter how fantastic you are at leadership, sales, recruiting, etc., a business coach offers insight, outside your field of vision. We all have blind spots holding us back from reaching our full potential, but we don't recognize them because we cannot see, what we cannot see.

"We need someone to guide us and hold us accountable to make sure we are reaching beyond our Comfy Cozy Comfort Zone and venturing out to the land where our Dreams live."

Because this industry is different from others, I recommend hiring someone with a Direct Sales background. Working with someone who understands the industry as well as the intricacies of the compensation plan without you having to explain it will save you time, money, and frustration.

For some of you, your **Upline** may be available to provide this role. They may have leadership skills and the time to work with you individually to help you build your business. This is an excellent option if it is available.

Sometimes when managing large teams or balancing busy **Schedules**, your **Upline** may not have the time to do one-on-one training. You may even find that your **Upline** doesn't have a strong leadership background. Leadership is learned through training, reading, coaching, and experience. They are probably doing the best that they can.

We should not fault those who don't already have experience. We all must learn, so don't start complaining. If you have used the excuse of not having a strong **Upline** as the reason you haven't done well in this business, you better **Pull Up Your Bootstraps (#PUYB)**, because this could get bumpy! It's time to **Quit Your Fitchin'**!

Chapter 5
QUIT YOUR FITCHIN'

"If you cannot be positive, then at least be quiet."
– Joel Osteen

I f you haven't read the **Fitchtionary** at the back of this book, then there may be a few terms that you are wondering about. **Quit your Fitchin'** (#QYF) is an expression I use as a reminder that complaining about your circumstances hinders your progress and stops you from flourishing into the entrepreneur you were meant to be. I highly recommend you engage in the #**BrightSide** philosophy.

The first way to break free from the negative mindset of complaining is to have a **PMA**.

PMA—Positive Mental Attitude

A **Positive Mental Attitude** is a choice. The world will whine and complain and try to drag you down. Those who are strong and want to grow, know that choosing to look at the #BrightSide of things will build their character and u_ ability to lead others.

> *"Only negative people choose to do business with,
> or to follow, a negative leader."*

Your attitude is your first line of defense against discouragement, disappointment and disaster. Unfortunate things are going to happen in your life. Preparing for them by strengthening your **PMA** will help you dodge the **Depths of Discouragement**.

One of the most notable attributes of someone with a **PMA** is that they strive to be a **Problem Solver**.

Problem Solvers vs. Problem Identifiers

One thing I try to tell my family, friends, and clients is to:

> *"Be a Problem Solver… not a Problem Identifier."*

A **Problem Solver (PS)**—looks at the problem with optimism and a commitment to finding a solution.

A **Problem Identifier (PI)**—notices everything that is wrong and then dumps it on someone else to resolve.

The Difference Between Problem Solvers
and Problem Identifiers

Problem Solvers	Problem Identifiers
Find **Great** Solutions	Complain
Create **positive** energy	Drain your energy
Look at the #**BrightSide**	Look for problems wherever they go
Spend time with people who **encourage** others	Hang around people who like to complain

As my Momma used to say, "Some people would complain if you gave them a Million dollars in pennies."

> **"Some people would complain if you gave them a Million dollars in pennies."**

A **Problem Identifier** would complain about the difficulty in handling that many coins, how dirty they are, and the time it would take to process them.

A **Problem Solver** would purchase an industrial coin counting machine, hire someone to convert it and haul it to the bank, and then lease the machine back to someone else in the business.

You may have encountered some of these **PI's** as customers, employees, or team members.

One rule I have for the **Problem Identifiers** of the world:

Rule #1:
If you want to complain,
you must provide me 3 possible solutions.

The possible solutions can be anything from **Obvious to Outlandish**. The objective is to create a culture of people engaged in finding solutions instead of passing the responsibility on to you.

If you want to influence others to think for themselves, and more importantly, to start looking for the positive in every situation, you need to be part of the change. So now is the time to ask yourself the hard question... are you a **Problem Solver**... or a **Problem Identifier**?

If you recognize your nature is that of a **Problem Identifier**, you may have gotten yourself marooned on **Fitchslap Island**. On the northwest part of the island, there is a place where the whiners and complainers get together to "share" their problems. You can see it on the map; it's called **Quit Your Fitchin' Cave**.

The **Problem Solvers** have a secret weapon that the **Problem Identifiers** don't know about. It is 3 simple words that change everything.

How Can I?

Problem Solvers don't say, "I Can't." Instead, they ask, "**How Can I?**"

The mind is a curious thing. If we tell it we CAN'T do something, it will stop searching for an answer. It's like closing a door on the possibilities. If we want it to search for answers, we need to pose a question instead of making a declarative statement. If you want to be a **Problem Solver**, ask yourself… "**How Can I?**"

To help you understand this concept, I'm going to share a story with you of how I transitioned from a **Hobbyist**, purchasing my products at a discount, to a consultant, operating a profitable business. I will show you the hurdles I faced and how I used **HCI (How Can I?)** to make my business thrive.

My "Accidental" Success Story

If you remember from **Chapter 2: My Story**, I shared how my **Upline** asked me to join the company, so I could get my products at cost. That is a far cry from becoming a Top-10 producer, so let me start at the beginning…

When you join a Direct Sales company, there is typically a kit that is sent to you that includes an assortment of products for you to demonstrate and sell to other people. I was particularly excited about the products that were on their way because I had previously been focused on the paper, pages, die cuts, stickers, etc. I didn't realize what a huge time saver the tools would be, so I hadn't invested in them. That was a big mistake.

The good news for me is that these tools were part of this goody box I was waiting for.

I got home from the office one day, scanning the porch to see if the box had arrived, and saw my neighbor approaching me from across the street. I walked over to meet her, as she was eyeing the box on my porch.

"Are you a Creative Memories Consultant?"

Honestly, I was dumbfounded. If you know me personally, you know it is very rare for me to be at a loss for words. My mind went blank for a second. I hadn't thought of myself as a consultant. After all, I was just an avid scrapbooker who found a permanent 30% off coupon that also came with an amazing deal of getting $500 worth of products for only $199. I was a bargain hunter, not a consultant.

I am embarrassed to share what tumbled out of my mouth next.

"Uh, yeah, I guess so."

WOW! A woman who started her first business at twelve years old cold calling, has built and sold multiple companies, and has dealt with very influential people, spits out, "Uh, yeah, I guess so." It was not my proudest moment as an entrepreneur, but her next words started a mindset shift …

"Are you holding workshops?"

Again, she didn't know that it was my brand-new consultant kit on the porch, nor did she know I had no real idea what she was talking about. Then she started speaking my language.

"You know, where people come over and PAY YOU to scrapbook with you."

#BOOM! There it was. Monetization. Making money doing something I LOVED to do with fun, like-minded people. I had the tools now, and since I had accumulated some inventory through my "Buy Me 2 Of Everything New!" **#BM2OEN** campaign, all I had to do was set up some tables and let people pay me to be there.

My entrepreneurial mind started kicking into gear, and I said,

"Yes, I'm actually doing one next Saturday. Would you like to come?"

For those of you judging me right now, that wasn't a lie. Just because I decided in that split second, doesn't change the fact that it is now on my mental calendar and that I'm committed to this event.

"Yes! I'm free, and I have a friend who loves to scrapbook too!"

Now we're talking! I haven't even opened my kit yet and I already have a workshop with two people coming! I know other people who scrapbook, so I'll just invite them to come, too. How hard can this be?

NOTE: If you are thinking, "My business doesn't have an opportunity to do paid events, classes, etc." you are probably wrong. I've taught people in dozens of different industries how to create a **Market Separator** that sets them apart from other representatives/companies and it often brings in an additional stream of income.

I went into the house and opened my kit, excited to play with my new toys. I realized I had to get busy and invite some other people before next Saturday to make the event a success. I shared the idea with my husband Terry, and as usual, he was very supportive, asking what he could do to help.

By the time I was done inviting, I had eight ladies coming to that first workshop. I didn't even know why, but I was really excited. When Saturday came, I set everything up, made food, got my tools out, and was ready to go! The workshop was scheduled from 2pm-6pm and suddenly, at 1:45pm, the **Bully** in my head started asking, "What if no one shows up?" I started to squirm and felt **Doubt** start to taunt me.

"Should I have done more?"

"Should I have called them to remind them?"

"Should I have announced that I was having food?"

Now remember, I have nothing riding on this except my own mental expectations, but in truth, NOBODY enjoys doing something they aren't successful at. We even try to shield our vulnerability with comments like,

"Hey, I didn't really want to do this anyway.", "I was just doing it because someone asked.", or "I could get more done in my scrapbooks alone anyway."

You probably know what I'm talking about. Whether it is a party or event that you were the hostess of, if you have invited people over, you have probably experienced that sinking feeling too. (Remember this when we talk about scheduling! ALL HOSTESSES are afraid of "Failing" or having no one show up. We need to address her **FEAR** and make her feel comfortable).

At 2:06pm, no one was there. I went upstairs to distract myself, so I wasn't sitting next to the door, like a dog waiting for a bone. My husband came into the bedroom and started this discouraging conversation,

Terry: "You sure went to a lot of trouble for no one to show up."

Me: [Stunned at his thoughtlessness, I just burst into tears.]

Terry: "What honey? What's wrong?"

Me: "REALLY? You have no idea?"

Terry: "For a guy, if no one shows up, we look at our buddy and go... 'Dude it's a bust.' And we watch TV or something."

Although in social settings it may be true that men are less concerned about attendance, they want people there too when business is involved.

At about 2:15pm, the doorbell rang. The ladies had all arrived and had even brought a couple additional friends. I had to fix my makeup, so I sent Terry downstairs to start greeting them and to get everyone settled. After all, I needed to come down looking carefree, right?

The event went really well, and I learned some very valuable things.

TIP: At every event, look for **Pain Points** you can solve or ways to improve. During this event, I recognized some problems and used the "**How Can I**?" question to come up with the solutions.

PAIN POINTS:

1. I want them to keep coming, so **how can I** get them to commit to the next event now?
2. People are often late, so **how can I** get them here on time?
3. Birds of a feather flock together, so **how can I** get them to invite their friends?
4. Making money means selling products too, so **how can I** make sure to have what they need before they get here?

Here was my solution. I made an announcement...

"OK Ladies, we have about thirty minutes left, and I wanted to let you know that I am having another workshop in two weeks. If you pay for it now, it will be $10 or $13 at the door.

I am doing something special at that one! I will have an "On Time Drawing!" Everyone who is here on time will get a chance to win a prize!

I know you all have friends who scrapbook too, so if you bring one of them with you, your next event is FREE!

And, to help you stay on top of your current projects, we will take a look at the catalog now and put your order together. That way, I can have your products here for the next event and you can be even more productive!"

The best solutions always include the **WIIFM (What's In It For Me?)** method. The **Pain Points** weren't just mine. We all like time for ourselves, and if we don't schedule it in advance, it likely won't happen. If it is on the calendar, you are less likely to schedule something else on top of it. And if you paid for it in advance, you have extra incentive to be there. I incentivized them to take care of themselves and help me to be more prepared for them. Simple ideas sometimes produce amazing results.

Some of you may be thinking those ideas are perfect and will implement them right away. Some of you might be saying, "Those ideas are so simple. I'm already doing those." I guarantee you, twenty plus years ago, these were cutting edge ideas. Remember, this was my first event and I had ZERO experience in this industry. Now, I have decades behind me.

The ideas get better and more profitable as I go along through the **#12Books12Months** series, so stick with me. This book is designed to give a foundation to those of you who are just starting in the Direct Sales Industry, and to add an extra layer of support for those of you who are seasoned veterans.

Quit your Fitchin' is a reminder that complaining is never the answer. The point of this story is that making excuses or complaining about our circumstances doesn't improve the situation. Being a **Problem Solver** who uses **"How Can I?"** will help you get to get to **#RockThatDream Ridge**.

Chapter 6

#RockThatDream Ridge

"You're off to Great Places! Today is your day!
Your mountain is waiting. So... get on your way!
– Dr. Suess

The entrepreneurial journey can be tough, and sometimes lonely, if we don't find like-minded travel companions. I wrote this series of books to provide you the map and access to a community of others who want to see you succeed.

Within **Fitchipelago**, there are several islands with various distinctions. Throughout the **#12Books12Months** series, you will visit each of them. Most entrepreneurs are in search of **Success Island**, with a desire to reach **#RockThatDream Ridge**. I want to help you get there as quickly as possible while avoiding unnecessary pitfalls.

There are several forms of transportation among the Islands, but one of the fastest and easiest is by helicopter. Our island hopper is called **Hope Helo**, and I want to take you on a quick, guided tour of **Success Island**.

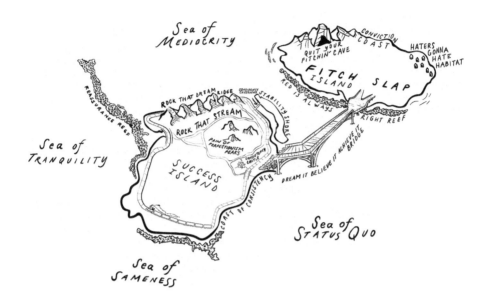

Success Island

From the air, you can see on the southwest side of the Island, the water is a gorgeous blend of blues and greens. Embracing the **Sea of Tranquility** on the west side, you will see **Reassurance Reef**, which boasts calm water and the most colorful and entertaining fish around. Continuing up the west side of the Island, you will find **#RockThatDream Ridge**, which is the home of a breath-taking, 360-degree view of all of **Fitchipelago**, called the **Pinnacle of Peace**.

Just to the east of the Ridge, you will find **Pain of Perfectionism Peaks.** This is the place where many entrepreneurs get stuck when they try to navigate the terrain alone. At the base of the mountain, nestled between the Ridge and the Peaks, you can see **#RockThatStream** with its clean, fresh water flowing into **Creativity Creek.** On the northeast side of the Island, you will find **Confidence Causeway,** which is the conduit to **Stability Shore.**

The next highlight of our bird's eye view of the Island is the expansive **Dream it, Believe it, Achieve it Bridge** that separates the **Sea of Mediocrity** from the **Sea of Status Quo.** It is the only footpath that connects to **Fitchslap Island.**

Continuing down the southeast side of the Island, you will see the pristine white beaches on the **Coast of Consistency**.

#RockThatDream Ridge

As we finish our first pass of the Island, we drop down to a lower altitude to take another look and become strategic on how to get to **#RockThatDream Ridge**. There are only two access roads headed there. One is clearly faster than the other, with a near straight shot across the Island to the base of the mountain. The other road repeatedly zig-zags across the area, including miles of twists and turns through the mountain range.

The road to the east, is unusually quiet with very little traffic and few cars. The road to the west has a lot of traffic and hazards that are slowing everyone down. We have the street map of the ground, but this aerial view provides a new perspective of why people are choosing to take the long way around.

The curvy road is easily accessed from the main streets. The straight road, on the other hand, starts half a mile away from the main thoroughfare with no obvious access point. Something is clearly in the way, but you will need to view it at ground level to identify if it is an obstruction, or something just hindering the view.

You sketch out your aerial view on how to find both locations from the heliport, so you can investigate the fastest way to **#RockThatDream Ridge** once you land.

Directions:

The Long Route: Head east on **Sales Street** through the main part of town. Stay left as it winds through the outer areas. Eventually, you will end up at the base of the mountains and will continue to follow that road through the range until you arrive at the base of your destination.

The Direct Route: Head north on **Dream It Drive**. Make a right on **Believe It Blvd,** and then take a quick left on **Achieve It Avenue**. Immediately, off to the right, you will see what is obscuring the access road.

As you approach the area, you locate the wall of vegetation that is blocking the visibility from the street. Upon closer review, you notice there is a sign peeking out of the trees, so you get out to take a closer look.

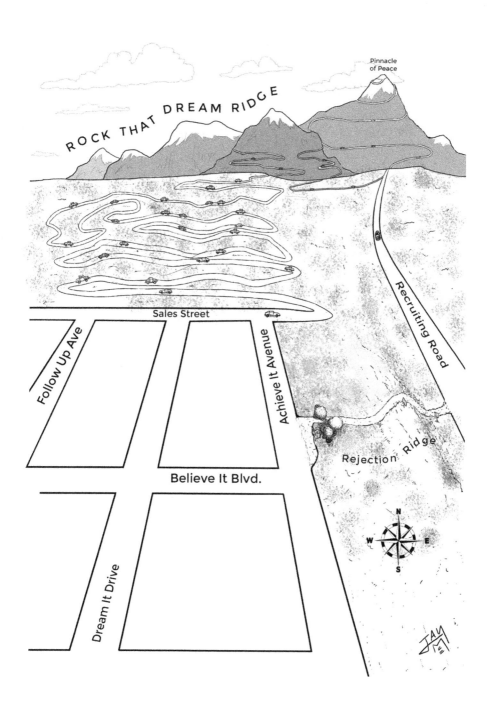

Tearing away the overgrown vines from the bottom, you read the street sign: **Rejection Road**. (No wonder people stopped using this access road.)

The sign is so dirty that you almost miss the words at the top. You use your hand to try to wipe away the caked-on mud to make out the word, **FEAR**.

With a little more effort, you wipe off the rest of the debris blocking your view to reveal the name on the sign—**FEAR of Rejection Road**.

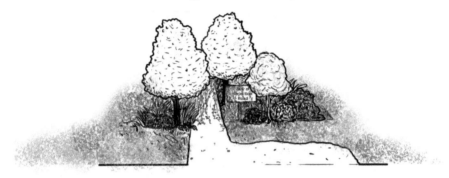

You know from your aerial surveillance that the distance between this opening and the road you are looking for is very short. You decide to take a chance and work your way through the overgrowth to get a ground level view of what is on the other side.

Navigating your way through the brush and trees only takes a minute. You notice another sign about one quarter mile down the road, and you hurry towards it. It too is covered in dirt, but you can make out the name **Rejection Ridge**. The ridge looks scary from this side, but having had that aerial vantage point, you know there is a soft slope on the other side that leads right onto the road you have been looking for.

Continuing on for that last quarter mile, you can see another sign up ahead. Next to the well-paved and rarely traveled road, the sign reads: **Recruiting Road** and the mystery is solved.

> ### *"The easiest way to get to #RockThatDream Ridge is on Recruiting Road."*

I understand your **FEAR** because I had to face mine too. Let me tell you about my journey and how I got to the top.

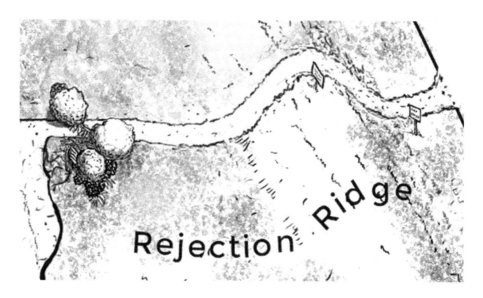

Rejection Ridge

My Journey

We have already determined that I am a new product junkie. (Remember **#BM2OEN?**) When new products came out, I had to have them right away. Fast forward a couple months. I received a postcard in the mail about a Regional Convention in my area. I wasn't interested in attending until I saw: **NEW PRODUCT GOODY BAG** for all participants. That changed everything, and I registered right away.

When the day finally arrived, I headed to the hotel and went straight to the registration table to pick up my products. My plan was to leave right afterwards, so I could start playing with my new toys.

Yes, you heard me right. (I say this with my head hung down in proverbial shame.) It's true. I was only there for the goody bag.

NOTE: There is a happy ending, since without this little episode, I wouldn't have written this book, so hold back your judgment and read on.

When I checked in, I was handed a name tag and some other materials, but no goody bag. I asked the girl behind the counter where I should pick it up.

"Oh, those are handed out after the speaker."

I was incredibly disappointed but chose the **#BrightSide**. I would talk to people, make some new friends, and see if I could discover some new scrapbooking tips.

Most of these ladies were struggling with the same **Pain Points** I originally had.

1. Getting people to events.
2. Getting them there on time.
3. Selling products.

I shared what I had been doing, and they were impressed and excited. I was fairly new in this industry, and I was doing more in sales per month than some of these eight to nine-year veterans.

Some of them suggested that I should be speaking at the convention. I laughed, thinking to myself, "I am just here for the goody bag." (I know, I know… I don't feel like that anymore.)

As time crawled along, I wondered when the speaker was going to start. Admittedly, due to my impatience, it seemed like forever. But she was worth the wait. As she started her speech, her voice cracked and cut in and out, and I had to really focus to understand what she was saying. It turns out, she had gotten sick and lost her voice, but was incredibly committed to delivering the message. I am convinced, the Lord put her there that day to speak to me.

Her beaming smile had me engaged from the start, but it was her story of trials that she turned into triumph that made me forget about the precious goody bag I had been anxiously waiting for.

Her name was Lisa Klaassen and her words pierced my heart in a way I cannot explain.

"If you aren't sharing this business with people you care about, you are being selfish." – Lisa Klaassen

---

I felt something wash over me at that moment as I realized, this was all about me. I wasn't treating this as a business or an opportunity for others, because I thought of it as a hobby. Lisa's words not only changed my perspective, but she actually changed my life.

When I arrived, I was a **Hobbyist** on a mission to get my new products. When I left, I was an entrepreneur prepared to operate a profitable business.

I filled out a "Go for the Goal" card to be a Unit Leader in 90 days. Back then, that was fairly unheard of— not because it couldn't be done, but because it typically took people around a year to achieve that level of success.

I will be honest. I didn't achieve it in 90 days. I actually did it in 33, and I didn't really try. I simply asked everyone one simple question…

"Just out of curiosity…"

Recruiting itself can be a scary thing, just like approaching the jungle-like opening in front of **FEAR of Rejection Road**. What if people say "No"? What if they think I'm pushy? The **FEAR** stops us before we ever open our mouths.

I would love to say that I came home from that event with the excitement and determination to make that goal of Unit Leader in 90 days, but I didn't. I was inspired while I was there, but when **FEAR** got a hold of me, my list of excuses **not** to recruit provided me a temporary distraction from that goal.

I realize this isn't what some of you may want to hear, but it is the truth. I wasn't looking for another business. I already had one that kept me really busy, and as you know, I wanted to stay home with my son. At the time, I didn't recognize this as the answer to my prayers.

By this time, my workshops had grown and required me to do two per month. Always looking to maximize my time and solve additional **Pain Points**, I started doing **Back to Back** events. On Friday night, **Midnight Madness** from 6pm-12am and Saturday 2pm-6pm.

This resolved my **Pain Point** of setting up and breaking down twice a month. The **Midnight Madness** event provided an alternate time for people with busy Saturdays. It also made it easier on spouses watching the children, since the kids were in bed most of the time mom was away.

On Friday night, things were going great at the workshop, I was demonstrating the new products and taking orders as usual. Suddenly, I heard this little voice in my head. It was Lisa Klaassen with her signature "Open Your Mouth" saying, "If you're not sharing this business… you're being selfish". Ugh, alright.

The pressure of writing down the "Go for the Goal" and holding myself accountable really put the pressure on. When I reminded myself of Lisa's words, I had a choice to make: encourage myself into action or drown out my goals with my excuses.

In an effort to quiet the internal dialogue and keep myself out of the "**Selfish Zone**", I decided to ask one of my guests a simple question. I walked up to Cheryl in the kitchen as she was getting a snack and casually started this conversation.

> **Me:** "**Just out of curiosity**, have you ever thought about doing something like this?"
>
> There, I said it. She can shut me down and tell me I'm crazy, but I didn't ask **if** she wanted to do it. I simply asked if she had **ever thought about it**. Her answer shocked me, and I probably had to peel my chin off the floor.
>
> **Cheryl:** "I was wondering if you were ever going to ask me. I didn't think you thought I could do it."
>
> It had never occurred to me that others were looking to me to see their own potential.
>
> It took me a moment to find my words through the rush of things buzzing around in my head, but I regained my bearings.
>
> **Me:** "Well, let's remedy that right now."
>
> I pulled out the paperwork and the first person I ever asked signed up to be on my team.

Cheryl is the perfect example of why you should never prejudge who would be interested in your business. She was a young mother of four, and at the time, she was very pregnant with her fifth. She was honestly the last person I thought would want to start a business.

NOTE: In case you didn't catch the symbolism here, that was my trip through the underbrush, facing **FEAR of Rejection Road** and staggering across **Rejection Ridge**. It was scary until I did it. Then I realized, the **FEAR** held no power, except in my mind. I arrived safely at the base of **Recruiting Road.**

Cheryl's reasons for wanting to join the team were completely different than mine. She wanted to get out of the house, have adult conversations, and contribute to her family, both inside and outside the home. Without Lisa's reminder at that convention, Cheryl may never have started. Or she may have signed up with the first person that asked her. The perception that someone Believes in you is a powerful thing and should never be underestimated.

I decided at that moment that no one would ever wonder again, if I believed in them. They may say "Yes", they may say "No", but they would never wonder if I thought they could do it.

There is a lot more to the story, but the short version is before the next workshop, I had:

- Recruited 6 people.
- Met our unit volume requirement.
- Promoted to title of Unit Leader.

NOTE: *It was Unit Manager at the time, but shortly thereafter changed to Leader, so I use that term instead.*

The moral of the story is to "Open Your Mouth!" and ask everyone, "**Just out of curiosity…**" You may be pleasantly surprised.

Chapter 7

GETTING YOUR FAMILY ON BOARD THE NEW BUSINESS BUS

"Family is not an important thing, it's EVERYTHING."
– Michael J. Fox

One of the most difficult parts of starting a business is having a solid support system to keep you encouraged and focused on success. Your family is your first line of defense. They will be there to celebrate your victories and to lift your spirits when things don't go as planned. We need them. Getting your family on board is a top priority.

As you know, when your family feels unappreciated, they tend to resent the time you spend building your business. Since your intention is to have your enterprise bless your family, I highly recommend you start showing them the rewards right away. Here are a few simple steps to help you do that.

Appeal to their GREED

The phrase "Appeal to their greed" means to find out what they want and find a way to help them get it. We all desire something, and we usually feel gratitude towards the people who help us get it. On the contrary, when we don't get what we want, and no one seems to care, we get frustrated and sometimes resentful.

Here is a scenario that might express those emotions in a silly, and yet possibly familiar way. The names and focal points may be different, but you will probably recognize the unsupportive behavior as something you, or a **Downline**, may have experienced before.

A Make-Believe Scene from the Fitch household

Hubby: "Honey, where are my socks?"

Me: "In your drawer."

Hubby: "No, they aren't."

Me: "Yes, they are."

Hubby: "Where? I can't find them."

Me: [Eyes rolling, walking to the drawer and pulling it open] "Right there."

Hubby: "Oh, they weren't there a minute ago."

Me: "REALLY?"

We don't need to go any further with that discussion, you get the point.

Add in Son…

Son: "Mommy!"

Me: "Hi Sweetheart. Mommy has to go out, but I'll be back soon."

Son: "No!" [Clutching my neck]

Me: "I'll only be gone a little while."

Son: "No!" [Still clutching my neck]

Me: "Aw sweetheart, Mommy loves you. I will be back in just a little bit."

Me: [speaking to Hubby] "Honey, can you take him for a while?" (Said with a begging smile so I'm not late)

Hubby: "Come on son, Mommy is leaving us again."

Me: "Awww come on, I'm running my business. It's for all of us."

Hubby: "We know, and we are not your business, so we don't get to see you. By the way, what's for dinner?"

Me: "I thought you were going to make something because I was going to be gone tonight."

Hubby: "Of course, I have to make dinner, take care of the kids, and do the laundry."

Me: "The socks were in your drawer!"

Hubby: "This time! What about all the other times?"

Me: [Frustration mounting and recognizing if I don't leave soon I will be late] I give out a heavy Sigh as I walk out the door.

Son: "Wahhhh! I want my mommy! Don't leave mommy!"

Of course, that scene was made up. But, I wonder if you've experienced something similar. I'm sure you agree that leaving the house in that discouraged state of mind would make it far less likely to produce the **Rock Star** results you are hoping for.

If we analyze the situation, address the **Pain Points,** and work on being a **Problem Solver**, we can change the way this scenario plays out.

Let's identify the **Pain Points**:

When we start a new business, or increase activity in our existing one, things change. Our spouse typically needs to take on more responsibility. Even when they agree to do that, if they don't feel appreciated, they may become resentful or just plain rebellious.

From our scenario above, the husband's complaints are the extra responsibilities he is taking on.

- Making dinner
- Watching the children
- Doing laundry (LOL)

The REAL **Pain Point** is lack of recognition and appreciation for the extra effort.

Think about that for a minute. Most of us don't mind taking on additional responsibilities, assuming we agreed to them in advance and are appreciated for participating. It is natural to feel upset when someone gives us responsibilities without asking us first. The same is true when they ask in advance, but then don't appreciate the effort we are providing.

IMPORTANT NOTE:
*If the thoughts running through your head are things like, "**It's about time they helped out.**" or "**I've been doing all that for a long time, it's his/her turn.**", I must caution you. Focusing on your expectations of how they should feel is a slippery slope. Complaining or justifying the way you feel, **isn't** going to resolve the problem. Remember the **WIIFM** Method. If support is what you really want, **Compassion** and **Empathy** are your best advocates.*

Children's complaints are usually based on wanting to feel important and knowing that they matter to their parents. In **Chapter 3: The "F" Words**, we talked about the **Lens** and the **Filter**. Your actions and reactions will form your children's self-esteem **Filter,** so this is your chance to help make it strong and durable. Spending time with you is important to them; but feeling valued as a member of the family is just as critical. When you set goals and you work towards them together as a family, it creates a bond that you can all enjoy together.

I have several ways for you to create calm out of the chaos, so let's start with something easy that effects them all. Let's talk food.

Meal Preparation

Whether or not you have been the primary food preparer in your home, your efforts here will be appreciated. It requires minimal time and produces maximum rewards.

Early on in my career, I became the "Crockpot Queen". My slow cooker and I are very close. The best of friends, really. She feeds my family a hot meal for me while I am away. I can trust her to deliver every time, which helps me satisfy a **Pain Point** in my family. (I have included my favorite recipe books on the resource page. **www.VickiFitch.com/DS101**)

Part of my weekly **Planning** is to review the calendar and plan our meals for the week. (Remember the **Rockstar Guide to Gettin' it Done**? That **Planning** section is in there so check it out!) After church on Sunday, we go grocery shopping and have lunch as a family. It's a very simple system, and it has served me well over the years. My family loves the food I make and to keep them excited, I even have them rate the meals on a scale of 1-10. That way, they are always getting the ones they enjoy.

I don't have to feel guilty about leaving, because they are fed and happy. I love that it is ready whenever they want to eat. There is usually enough left over for lunch the next day, which saves me time too. When everyone is on the same page, and working towards the same goals, you create an atmosphere of cooperation.

Choose the Rewards

Next, we want to find out our families' **Dreams**. We all have things we want. Some are small things we could supply weekly, like a special dessert or treat. Others take **Planning** and saving. It is important to find out what your family wants, and what they are willing to work towards.

For kids, it might be a new video game, bicycle, phone, or even a car, depending on their ages. For adults, it might be something like a night out with friends, new golf clubs, or season tickets to their favorite sports team. The items don't matter. What does matter is that you care enough to find out what they want and come up with a plan to make sure they get them.

It is also important to recognize that it may not be physical things that some of them are interested in. Perhaps having a picnic in the park, flying a kite, or playing hide-and-seek is what your kids really want. Oftentimes, we don't realize how much they crave our attention. They want time that is focused on them, not you, checking your email, answering the phone, or conducting business. Just focused family fun.

In order to find out, you need to sit down as a family and ask what they would consider exciting rewards. Ask about their favorite things and make a list. Here are some samples that have dollar values attached, as well as activities that are mostly free. This should get you started with some ideas for your own family.

NOTE: You will have different categories to celebrate based on your company's reward system. You'll notice there is a graduated scale that increases reward value based on the commission or bonuses you would be earning. Customize it to fit your business.

SAMPLE—Family Reward System

Goal	Reward
Recruit new Team Member	Ice Cream, Small Toy, Video game time
Every $300 Sales	$5 in Family Fund
$500 Event	Fast Food Outing or Picnic in the park
$1000 Event	Video Game or Family Game
Reaching Personal Best—Sales	$10 in Family Fund
Reaching Personal Best—Recruiting	Family Movie Night—At home or the theatre
Reaching Monthly Sales Goal	$15 in Family Fund
Reaching Monthly Recruiting Goal	$20 in Family Fund
Reaching Team Sales Goal	Family Dinner Out or Special Dinner at home.
Reaching Team Recruiting Goal	$50 in Family Fund
Promotion	Season Passes to a theme park

Consider using a portion of the **Family Fund** each month to invest in a family game or activity. The rest of the money that is earned can be accumulated for a family vacation or a home renovation. Putting in a treehouse, pool, or game room might appeal to your family! Let them **Dream**!

Keep it Fresh

It is important to keep the rewards fresh. For instance, when I recruited double digits every month, going out for ice cream lost its appeal. We had to adjust the **Rewards Chart** to keep it interesting.

Bonus Rewards & Opportunities

There are always times of the month or year that are extra busy. On those days, you can offer bonuses for cheerful participation. For instance, month end is typically a busy time. I often had to spend extra time on the phone to help the team process their paperwork or confirm they met qualifications for their incentives. Reminding my family about the Bonus Rewards kept them excited and cheering me on to do my job. We all get more motivated when there is something in it for us too.

Preparing your family in advance will help reduce any frustration by them getting caught off guard. Posting the dates on your family calendar or posting a count down on the refrigerator can make it fun. Helping them plan activities for those days or having something special they can only use during those times could be a real advantage!

Letting them earn Bonus Rewards or even money, depending on their age and ability, may provide you with extra help and them with extra motivation. Stamping literature, making reminder calls, entering data, or filling orders are easy things to offload while helping your family to build their entrepreneurial spirit.

Family Night

We had **Family Night** every Wednesday where we played games and had no outside distractions. It was an important part of our family bonding. More on that in *DS 201*.

Family Activity: You could create a Reward or **Dream Board** where you and your family can either take pictures out of a magazine or print them from the internet and place them on the board for the whole family to see. Keeping your goals in front of you is the first step to achieving them. It is also a fun way for your family to share the new things they are excited about.

Deliver the Rewards

Make a big deal out of putting money in the **Family Fund** whenever you earn it. You could even do a thermostat on your **Dream Board** showing them how close they are to earning the big prize you are saving up for.

Make sure that each week, there is always something to celebrate. If you didn't hold any events or make any sales, celebrate the amount of calls you made or new contacts you met. Keep your efforts in front of everyone and remember "small wins" keep everyone's eyes on the prize! Make sure they know how important they are to your businesses success!

NOTE: It is also important to reward yourself to keep **your** enthusiasm and excitement at its peak. *DS 201* will go into more details for you. Right now, we have to focus on the family, but know it is important to celebrate you!

No one enjoys a reward they earn that doesn't get delivered. That will create resentment. Set a specific time each week when you either count the money in the **Family Fund** or deliver the prizes for the week. Make it part of your family day/night so it becomes a regular habit everyone can look forward to.

So now you know how to "Get Your Family on Board the New Business Bus!" Be creative and BE CONSISTENT.

Chapter 8

THE QUEEN OF CONSISTENCY

*"We are what we Consistently do. Excellence
therefore is not an act, but a Habit."*
– Aristotle

You may have guessed by the title of this chapter that I have been dubbed the **Queen of Consistency**. My secret is not closely guarded. I created a method of transportation to get around **Success Island** and developed the special tracks for it to run on. Let me start by telling you about the **Habit Train**.

Habit Train

When I first came to the coast, there was no transportation to move freely around **Success Island**. Recognizing the need, I went to work on creating a railway system to provide the residents access to anywhere on the Island.

It was a massive project that required extensive **Planning**. First, I needed to outline where the track would be laid and identify how much material would be needed. Then I had to source the materials and create **Systems** to track them and make sure we had a constant supply. Next was developing **Procedures** on how each component would connect, and who would be responsible for each task. Following that was creating **Schedules** that secured timely material deliveries to avoid unnecessary delays. Grouping the **Systems, Procedures,** and **Schedules** together created **Routines,** which led to **Efficiency**. The result was exponential **Productivity**.

When you put all these railcars together, they form the **Habit Train.**

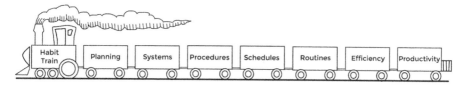

Now that you understand the basics of the **Habit Train**, you need to understand how it applies to your business, what the fuel source is, and how it is operated.

Auto Pilot

One of the keys to my success is creating the "auto pilot" of my business. **Auto Pilot** is the Conductor of the **Habit Train.**

When you do the same things consistently every day, they become habits. Once they are habits, you don't have to think about them anymore. They become part of your day, like brushing your teeth and eating your breakfast. The more consistent you are with a daily schedule, the easier your days, weeks, months, and years will become.

I have been doing the same routine for years. I get up before 5am, do my Bible Study and daily devotion. Next, I read my book of the month, so I can grow in my walk as a leader. Then, I put in 30 minutes on the treadmill, where I answer messages, catch up on podcasts, listen to audio books, or even watch a

TV show or news program. After that, I take a shower, get ready, throw a load of laundry in, and get my son ready for school.

It is the same thing every day. I don't have to plan that portion of my day out. It is predictable. My body knows what to do when I get up, so it requires less thinking and active engagement. This allows my mind to work on other, more important things, like coming up with creative ways to market my business.

Fueling the Habit Train

When you gather all the railcars together, **Planning**, **Systems**, **Procedures**, **Schedules**, **Routines**, **Efficiency** and **Productivity**, your **Habit Train** is ready for motion. Engage the **Auto Pilot**, and now you are ready to add the fuel.

"Momentum is the coal that keeps your train moving, and Consistency is the person shoveling it into the fire."

Momentum is the fuel source, but without **Consistency**, eventually you will run out of steam and your **Habit Train** will come to an unscheduled stop.

Consistency is the key for any entrepreneur. Setting a schedule that includes all the necessary activities for running your business is critical. Staying consistent with all your responsibilities, including the back-end activities like paperwork and phone calls, will keep your business **Momentum** moving forward.

The Power of a Habit

Being an entrepreneur for many decades has given me ample time to learn what makes me more productive and what distracts me from my goals. People are often astonished that I can run multiple companies, manage my family, serve my clients, volunteer my time, and still have time for myself. I will be honest. It hasn't always been **Easy**, but it is **Simple**.

In case that statement is confusing for you, let me break down the definitions of **Easy** vs. **Simple**.

Easy means without great effort. **Simple** means easy to understand.

It isn't **Easy** at first, because it does require effort. Putting together a consistent schedule of activities will require time and energy, until you master it and it becomes habit. Once something becomes a habit, you are free to use your energy to master a new task.

"CREATING
a habit is difficult,
MAINTAINING
a habit is easy."

It is **Simple**, because it is broken up into bite size, manageable pieces. When we look at our massive To Do list, it can be overwhelming. It is worse if we haven't written that list down. Trying to complete a list of things that are constantly swimming around in your head is a futile effort. It is like playing a game of Whack-A-Mole in the **Entrepreneurial Theme Park** (We will visit the **ETP** in *DS 201*)

It is imperative we capture our thoughts, organize them, and develop an execution strategy to complete them. Some are single, one-off items, but most of what we do each day has a consistent nature to it. When you create a productive habit from your daily activities, the number of things you can accomplish is astronomical.

Think about this series of books for instance. The **#12Books12Months** project wouldn't be possible if I didn't have a finely tuned scheduled, with ample time scheduled in to write, alongside all my other activities. Tackling any project requires time, effort, commitment, and focus.

Waking up without a plan each day on how to make the most of the time available would most likely leave me promising myself… *"I'll start tomorrow"*, instead of *"I will execute today."*

I recognize there are many of you reading this book that feel being constrained by a schedule would make you feel tied down. Remember that if YOU create your schedule and are adding in the things that are important to YOU, it is a different experience.

> *"YOU are the master of your schedule.*
> *What you do, or don't accomplish, is strictly up to you."*

The purpose of **Planning** and creating a **Schedule** is to get your **Habit Train** on the tracks. After that, add **Momentum** and **Consistency** to power it and you are ready to move forward to **#RockThatDream Ridge**. It isn't very far away, so let's build those tracks!

Laying the Tracks

Now that the **Habit Train** is ready to roll, it is time to lay the **RSG2GID** track.

RSG2GID

You probably figured out that **RSG2GID** (the **Rock Star Guide to Gettin' It Done**) is a compilation of all the information packed into the railcars on the **Habit Train.** The step-by-step organizational and time management system will serve as the tracks for it to run on. It is important you understand why it works by giving you another little sample of its power.

I plan my weekly schedule on Fridays by starting with what I call the **Non-Negotiables** for the week, including my morning routine and any appointments or meetings already scheduled. I then fill in the other activities and priorities using **Layering** and **Group Tasking** to allow for maximum **Productivity**. By **Planning** in advance, I can see any possible conflicts and make the appropriate adjustments. (If you want to increase your **Productivity** and create excellent habits, I recommend you get the **RSG2GID** at **www.VickiFitch.com/DS101**.

In addition to my **Weekly Planning**, I have days scheduled for **Monthly**, **Quarterly**, **Semi-Annual**, and **Yearly Planning** as well.

Why do I invest this time into **Planning**? So I can stay consistent.

- **Consistent** with my goals so I can measure and adjust them appropriately.
- **Consistent** with my **Livestreaming** schedule so clients and potential clients can see that I am committed to my craft.

- **Consistent** in my exercise **Routines** to keep my energy level up and my mind sharp.
- **Consistent** in my education so I never find myself stuck and stagnant because I let an important part of my growth slip through the cracks.
- **Consistent** with my schedule so I don't have to put so much time and effort into thinking, "What's next?"

Consistency is what tells my team members that I am there to support them, and that they can count on me. It is also what tells my coaching clients I am here for the long haul which provides the **Confidence** that they can develop these skills too.

"Consistency is more than a word. It is a way of life."

Have you ever tried to order something from a friend who was in a Direct Sales company, and found when you called to place an order they "weren't doing that anymore?" They are now in a different **DS** company and are eager to share their new products with you. The next time you see them, they may have jumped ship and gone on to something new yet again. (I call these people **DSA Hoppers**, which we will talk about in *DS 201*)

Why did this happen and why is it so common? It may be due to the fact they didn't love the product or company that they were representing. But oftentimes, it is because they weren't making money due to their lack of consistency.

Consistency gets you through the difficult times when you are sick, tired, or frustrated. Your **Auto Pilot** kicks in on the **Habit Train**, and you just do what needs to be done. You don't have to actively think about it. You automatically make those calls, place those orders, and show people, including yourself, you can be counted on.

Do YOU Trust YOU?

Developing the **Habit Train** was the first step in connecting the community; but laying the **RSG2GID** tracks to run on was the golden ticket.

Some of my friends say you can set your watch by what activity I am doing on a certain day. I am actually not that rigid, because I do move things around when I need to adjust. But, my consistency and the habits I've included in the **Rock Star Guide to Gettin' It Done** assure me the things that are moved, get back on the schedule, and don't get lost in the shuffle.

Most people equate consistency with trustworthiness. When people are consistent, you can count on them and when you can count on them, you tend to trust them. We want clients and customers to feel that way about us, but we also want to feel that way about ourselves. If you have struggled with being consistent, you have also probably struggled with your self-esteem. It stands to reason if you can't trust yourself to complete the tasks you are responsible for; your confidence will suffer. When your confidence suffers, so will your **Productivity**.

"When your Productivity increases, so will your profits."

As a leader, you want to set a profitable example for your team. That requires you to be productive, and the best way to do that is to have a schedule and to set boundaries. If you are prepared to implement these changes and hop aboard the **Habit Train**, your arrival at **#RockThatDream Ridge** will be faster than you ever thought possible.

Setting Boundaries

Throughout **Success Island**, there are Train Depots to pick up and drop off passengers at various locations around the Island. These stops are **Scheduled** to allow passengers adequate **Planning** time. The locations and times of operation are set in advance. Everyone must respect them, or they will miss the train and be left behind.

Part of consistency is setting effective boundaries for you and your business. That means setting specific times to work with team members and clients. One of the fastest ways to get burned out is by letting your business run **you,** instead of **you** running your business. That is why scheduling and time blocking are crucial elements to your success.

Many entrepreneurs confuse operating a business with running a 24/7 mini mart. Don't fool yourself into thinking that in order to succeed, you must be available all the time to handle anything that comes up, whenever it comes up.

Just like the Train Depots, we need to have set hours for our businesses. One of the main things I see consultants doing is taking client or team calls at any time of the day or night. You can be flexible with your hours, but be specific and consistent. Set clear boundaries and expectations and teach your team to be resourceful from the start. They will emulate this behavior with their own teams and will have the **Confidence** to run their businesses on their own.

The best thing you can do to support your team and yourself, in addition to your consistency, is to become an **Expert** in your field. In the next chapter, I will talk about my experience in a brand-new industry, and how I became the go-to person for questions, even though most of the people asking the questions had much more experience in that industry than I did.

There are people who avoid the word **Expert**. They are worried other people will **Believe** they are cocky or are trying to overstate their skill set. Some even say **Expert** is a dirty word. Well if it is, let me talk dirty to ya!

Chapter 9

EXPERT IS NOT A DIRTY WORD

"The Expert in anything, was once a beginner."
– Helen Hayes

As you probably already know, if you have watched any of my daily **Livestreams**, heard my podcasts, or had any interactions with me, I am a G-Rated Girl.

Although the intro to this chapter may sound a bit provocative to some of you, I want to help you understand:

- What an **Expert** is
- Why people are afraid of them
- Why you might be afraid to admit you are an **Expert**
- How to become one and **OWN IT**

First, let's start off with the definition of an **Expert** as defined by Google.

ex·pert—A person who has a comprehensive and authoritative knowledge of or skill in a particular area

As that definition stands, does it describe you?

This isn't the time to be modest. If it does describe you, then you should start owning that title right now without worrying about other people's opinion of the word. Be honest and bold about your skills and who you are. There is a difference between **Confidence** and **Cockiness**. We compare these twin brothers in *Evict the Bully in Your Head.*

I am an **Expert** in the Direct Sales industry. Do these qualifications meet the litmus test of the definition?

> *I have been in the industry for twenty years, Top 10 Sales & Recruiting Internationally for more than a decade.*

Does that qualify me as having **a comprehensive and authoritative knowledge of or skill in this particular area**? The obvious answer is yes, and owning that distinction is important.

If your concern is the length of time it takes to become and **Expert**, you should understand you don't have to master an entire industry. You can start with expertise in your company or a specific line of your company's products. As your education grows, your areas of expertise will expand. This chapter is dedicated to helping you OWN who you are, and to help you recognize and celebrate your skills. Let's talk about how to do that.

Commit to a PMA

We talked about the power of a **Positive Mental Attitude (PMA)** in **Chapter 5: Quit Your Fitchin'**, but let's address how it will assist you in developing your expertise. There is a lot of information to learn about your industry, and you must recognize that you aren't going to learn it all at once. Your goal should be to learn as much as you can, so you can serve your clients and team members with the best skill set you have to offer. Becoming an **Expert** is the byproduct of your efforts. It is the result of your actions toward excellence.

By now, you must know that my tagline is "**Dream it, Believe it, Achieve it!**" When you choose to **Believe** in yourself, you may encounter some resistance from others who are determined to keep swimming in the **Sea of Mediocrity**. If you stay adrift there too long, you may find yourself washed up on shore, stranded on **Fitchslap Island**. (I will share more about that Island in another book, but for now, let's focus on developing your expertise so you can *#RockThatDream*.)

Follow the Leaders

When my husband Terry was still my fiancée, he invited me to my first sales and leadership conference. I met Brian Tracy, Jim Rohn, Tom Hopkins, and a host of other inspirational people. That seminar was when I realized, that something was missing in my life. I had a thirst for knowledge that was unquenchable, but I had no clear path to where I was going or how I would get there.

After hearing these orators speak, I started consuming their content any way I could. I knew I wanted to grow, so I purchased their books and tapes. (Yes, tapes! LOL Audio cassettes and VHS.) I started listening to them every morning on my drive to work, creating a culture of learning and understanding. I didn't realize there was so much out there to inspire me! Up to this point, I had always relied on inspiring myself.

There was no internet at the time, so attending seminars, reading, listening to tapes, or watching videos were the only resources available. (I know, I am dating myself. But hey, if I can do it without the internet, IMAGINE what you can do now!) The more I listened, watched, and read, the more I was inspired. I realized that I hadn't been **Dreaming** about my future and what I really wanted. I didn't understand or recognize the power of a **Dream** and how it could be such a catalyst for success.

At the time, I was not thinking of being an Author, Keynote Speaker, or International Business Consultant. My focus was on my current job, my team, and my community. I always knew I wanted to write a book, but I wasn't sure why or how to go about doing it. It was more of a fleeting thought than a **Dream** or goal.

The speakers who I had been introduced to started molding my thinking, encouraging me to **Dream** and ditch any limiting beliefs. I was free to **Believe** I could literally do anything if I wrote it down and put an action plan together.

I spent hours thinking about what I really wanted and writing down all of my goals. I then put a detailed action plan, including manageable, bite size, measurable pieces. (As Tom Hopkins says, "**Reduce it to the Ridiculous.**") I named this course **Dreaming into Achieving** and went on a mission to share it with my staff. Teaching them to **Believe** in themselves and showing them how to create an action plan was a gift I wanted to share. There was obvious power in turning our **Dreams** into goals.

"Goals are just Dreams, with a deadline." – Napoleon Hill

I consumed books and sought out knowledge like no other time in my life. I read books on relationships, people, learning styles, psychology, training, sales, motivation, etc. You name it, I was consuming it. I felt like I had a whole new arsenal of information to guide and support others, while I was growing myself.

I also realized I had a natural talent. Not for "selling", but for caring and connecting, which made me an excellent sales person. For me, it wasn't about "closing a sale", it was about being a **Problem Solver** and finding solutions to other people's **Pain Points**.

When I sold my bookkeeping and tax company to run a division of a publicly traded company, I started reading industry publications and taking classes in water chemistry, concrete, substrates, concrete repair methods, epoxy injection, etc. I wanted to understand the industry, participate in conversations, and ask intelligent questions of the **Experts**.

Guess what happened?

Some of those industry **Experts** started coming to me to ask questions. Why? Because I was learning the entire industry, not just a specific area of it. As a result, others started to seek out my opinions, information, and contacts.

My point in sharing this is to tell you that it doesn't matter how long you have been in an industry. If you ask good questions and immerse yourself in learning, people will eventually see your expertise and respect you as a reliable source of industry information.

My six-month experience superseded the knowledge of some ten and twenty-year veterans, not in their specific trade, but in the industry as a whole.

You shouldn't be intimidated by the length of time someone has been in your industry, assuming you will never be "as good as they are", because that isn't true. As a matter of fact, if they are average people, you will likely surpass them if you choose to invest in yourself and apply your knowledge.

When my husband and I left that company to start our own construction company, I was ahead of the curve. I may not have had my contractor's license, but I bet with a little prep work I could pass the test for a C8 (concrete) and a D6 (concrete specialty) license. Why? Because I had been learning from the best.

People enjoy talking about themselves and their career. They also usually like to share advice. I listened to their wisdom, asked great questions, and shared what I knew would help others. The result: I became well-respected in the industry, and someone others sought out to connect with.

Use Your Resources

Jim Rohn, who was Tony Robbins' mentor, was a huge proponent of expanding your knowledge as often as you could. He was considered a modern-day philosopher, and I personally loved consuming his content. I started my leadership journey by listening to his words of wisdom and applying them to my life. When I followed his suggestions, things changed in ways that I hadn't imagined possible. His "Vitamins for the Mind" were a daily dose of advice, inspiration, and encouragement.

Mr. Rohn, God rest his soul, was the primary influence in me recognizing the true power of vocabulary.

One of his simple, yet incredibly important reminders, was that everyone should have a library card. At that time, only 3% of the population even bothered to obtain access to the most valuable FREE resource available to them, and I suspect that statistic is even lower today.

Former First Lady Laura Bush believed that to be true as well.

"I have found the most valuable thing in my wallet, is my library card." – Laura Bush

When I originally heard Jim Rohn speak about this, I didn't have a library card myself. After graduation, I had the ill-conceived notion that I had no need for books unless they were for pleasure reading. It is sad that my perspective was so limited, but I can't blame myself for what I didn't know. I can choose to share what I have learned to inspire others to grow. Just as Jim Rohn did for me, I want to inspire others to engage in this opportunity sooner than I did. The **#12Books12Months** series is designed to not only encourage that behavior, but to provide a fun way to deliver relevant information to youth and adults alike. I want to inspire all of you to become thought leaders and to pursue becoming the best YOU, you can be!

University on Wheels

Experts don't just happen overnight. It takes time, education, and training to get there. Reading, understanding, and becoming a committed student of your industry requires you to proactively think about it and find time to develop your expertise.

With the ample supply of resources available, there are few reasons to prevent you from excelling in any field. I know some of you don't like to read, and some of you feel you don't have much time to read. Utilizing the "**Mobile Classroom**" or "**University on Wheels**" concept is a solution most people can integrate into their daily lives. (If you need a list of books I recommend, you can find a link on my website **www.VickiFitch.com/DS101**.)

Audio Books

In *Dare to Dream, Work to Win*, Dr. Tom Barrett recommends you use the "**Nooks & Crannies**" of your day. Listening to audio books every day allows me to fill those "**Nooks & Crannies**" by **Layering** in an audio book while I do any number of mundane tasks. Walking on the treadmill, opening mail, making lunches, folding laundry, driving in the car, etc. When you make a habit of listening when you have time, you will be surprised how much new information you acquire, or how many additional skills you master.

Some of you may have used expensive options for your audio listening in the past, or possibly thought it was out of your budget. At the time of this writing, I am currently in love with a FREE app called Overdrive. It connects with your local libraries and allows you to virtually check-out up to ten titles at once and put thousands on a waiting list. At the present time, this service is completely free.

A physical library card isn't required so there is no need to have to leave your home to gain access. You can request an electronic library card online. Since the books automatically check themselves back in, there will never be any late fees or costs associated for forgetting to return an overdue book. It is an excellent way to increase your expertise and expand your knowledge base into areas that might help your business to grow and your life to improve.

For the few of you out there who don't have a smart phone or access to the internet, the old-fashioned way of checking out material is currently still available. By the time you read this, that may have completely gone away, but there will probably still be some free resources available. When I hear of new options or additional ways to help you excel, I will post them on my website at **www.VickiFitch.com/DS101**. I recommend you check back there often.

We already discussed **Scheduling** in several chapters, but I wanted to remind you that this activity should be one of your **Non-Negotiables** on the **Habit Train** if you are serious about becoming an **Expert**.

Learn from the Experts

This chapter is full of detailed information on understanding what expertise really is, and how to make sure you start working on becoming an **Expert** a little every day. True expertise is knowledge + experience. Your experience can be first hand or learned from someone else. This series of books is my effort to provide you some of that experience, and to provide you the benefit of 20/20 hindsight.

One of my biggest mistakes

As I mentioned in **Chapter 4: Planning and Preparation**, one of my biggest mistakes was NOT hiring a business coach in the beginning. As you know, I didn't get into the industry as a business. I was a **Hobbyist** who wanted to get my products at cost. Once I caught the vision, I still didn't understand that I needed someone who had already been to **#RockThatDream Ridge** to guide me there safely. Remember, I had already built and sold a successful company, and my second business was doing extremely well. I never had a mentor to share things with me, so it just never occurred to me, which is why I am telling you. If I had invested in that resource in the beginning, I am certain I would have made it to the Ridge ten times faster than I did, and the ride wouldn't have been as bumpy.

Here is a checklist to keep you growing and on top of your entrepreneurial game:

- **Expert** is NOT a dirty word.
- **Experts OWN IT** when it comes to their abilities, embrace where they are on the journey, and commit themselves to daily progress.
- **Experts** focus on having a **PMA—Positive Mental Attitude.** It sets them apart from others and keeps their minds open for learning and growing in their industry.
- **Experts** learn to be good leaders by **following Great leaders.**
- **Experts** write down their **Dreams** and turn them into goals by assigning deadlines.
- **Experts** are **Problem Solvers** who look for ways to solve **Pain Points.**
- **Experts spend time with other Experts** to learn and grow.
- **Experts utilize the resources available** to them.
- **Experts** read every day and obtain a **library card** to gain free access to a wealth of knowledge.
- **Experts** recognize the value of a **University on Wheels** to help them expand their knowledge and use **Layering** to help them grow as a person, an entrepreneur, and a leader.
- **Experts** invest in themselves and hire a guide to lead them to **#RockThatDream Ridge.**

So now that you know how to work towards being an **Expert,** let's help you with the fundamentals of this industry.

Chapter 10
THE "HOW TO" OF DIRECT SALES

"The only thing keeping you from getting what you want,
is the story you keep telling yourself about why you can't have it."
– Tony Robbins

T he purpose of this chapter is to help you understand some of the "How To's" of Direct Sales that won't be found in your **NCT (New Consultant Training)** manual. The intention is to provide you with perspective and understanding of how to think differently so you can truly *#RockThatDream*! Let's do a quick check of where you are with your current business.

Direct Sales Checklist
_____ Joined a company I Love!
_____ Watched all the videos recommended by the company/my **Upline**
_____ Watched a live demonstration of my **Upline** or someone who was recommended

_____ Watched a virtual demonstration by my **Upline** or someone who was recommended

_____ Chosen a business book to read fifteen minutes a day (this one counts!)

If you checked off all those items, you are ready to set sail for **Success Island**. If not, schedule in some time every day to do those things, while you add the rest of what you'll learn from this book. You already know that the **Rockstar Guide to Gettin' It Done** will be your best friend as you try to create an effective schedule that will continue moving your business forward. If you haven't checked it out yet, that should be at the top of your To Do list.

K.I.S.S.

You have probably heard of the **K.I.S.S.** method. (**K**eep **I**t **S**imple **S**weetheart— Yes, I changed the last word—I **Believe** in positive self-talk.) My goal is to help you keep your business simple. A lot of people overcomplicate it and get caught in the **Ocean of Overwhelm**. This book is designed to give you the basics with the insight and understanding of the industry. Each additional book in the series will add on an additional layer of support and understanding for you to move through gradually.

Let's start with something simple…

The Evidence Check

My friend and early mentor, Nyra Carranza, told me about the **Evidence Check**. It is simple. Ask yourself this question every day before you leave the house.

"If you were arrested for being a consultant at your company, would there be enough evidence to convict you?"

You should always have at least five pieces of **Evidence** on you at all times. That helps build both conscious and subconscious awareness of your connection to your brand.

Here are some ideas of "**Evidence**":

- Logo'd apparel or gear
- Pens
- Business Cards
- Catalogs
- Company pins, emblems, or name tags
- Industry Specific Products (Clothing, jewelry, handbags, shoes, etc.)

If your company is new or has limited logo item options, I have found stickers to be the easiest, most cost-effective way of creating **Evidence**.

When I was with my first **DS** company, I had so much **Evidence**, I was a walking conviction waiting to happen. When I went to the gym, I had stickers on all my locker room supplies— hair dryer, shampoo, conditioner, bottle of shower gel, make up, etc. In addition, I had a gym bag, make-up bag, towel, and workout shirt with my logo embroidered on it.

Market Separator

In the Direct Sales Industry, there are thousands, tens of thousands, or hundreds of thousands of people doing the same thing as you do. Therefore, we need to give consumers a reason to choose YOU, over all the other people who can supply them with the same products and/or services. Building custom packages with bonuses or including extra incentives like recipes, instruction sheets, or special video links, can all provide you an exclusive edge over your competition.

Example: A major **Pain Point** in the traditional scrapbooking industry was **Time**.

Most clients felt challenged with finding enough time to work on their projects. In addition to working on their albums, there was usually set up and clean up time needed as well.

Since I had the same **Pain Point** regarding my own projects, I came up with an incredibly effective solution that allowed me to stay current on my albums in only 15 minutes a day. That was part of my **Market Separator**. It had several layers to it, which I will explain in a moment.

A second **Pain Point** was **Space**.

I created my own custom collection of supplies that only needed a 2' x 2' area on a table and a 3' x 2' footprint on the ground beside it. It was a set up that was on wheels and could easily be rolled into a corner or closet, so it wasn't an eye sore when guests came over. It also gave the dining room table back to the family.

My **15 Minute Focus** class alleviated both the **Time** and **Space Pain Points** with a specific set of products that I used to be efficient with my scrapbooking. I charged each person $15 per session, but I gave the classes away for FREE with the purchase of the collections. This provided them the hands-on instruction they needed to become confident in their own skills.

Being a **Problem Solver** and resolving my own concerns created a **Market Separator** that grew my business exponentially.

Bundling

I created custom collections by **Bundling** the products that were needed to quickly and easily perform the tasks I would be demonstrating. There were 3 options available, each adding on an additional layer of savings: Time, Space and Money. When all 3 packages were purchased together, they offered the greatest value and an abundance of rewards.

When you can

- Solve your clients' **Pain Points**
- Cater to their needs
- Personalize your service
- Save them time and money

You will create a loyal customer with nearly guaranteed repeat sales.

The added benefit of them being more productive was that they completed more scrapbooks, which meant they purchased more products. (This is one of the advantages of having a consumable product.) It was a win-win, and the combination of excitement and **Productivity** became the perfect formula for success. It increased my sales, scheduling, and recruiting.

Just to share with you what a difference having specialty bundles made in my sales, let me share a couple of facts with you. At the time,

The average purchase per person at a Beginning Class was $50.

My average was **over $450**. That is **900% more than the average consultant.**

The average total sales at a Beginning Class for a representative was $300.

My average was **over $2000**. That is **over 500% more than the average consultant.**

My sales per person were almost 10 times what the average consultant sold at a Beginning Class

I would only accept 4-6 people at my Beginning Classes to provide customized attention and care. Other reps were inviting 10-20 people or more to each event. Their attendance was higher, but their sales were significantly lower. They weren't able to adequately service that number of guests and were often losing sales when people had to leave. **Bigger isn't always Better!**

Before you tell me that there is nothing different about your business and no way to separate yourself, I am 100% confident that you can. I want to encourage you to start thinking with the **"How Can I?"** mindset.

How Can I?

In **Chapter 5: Quit Your Fitchin'**, I introduced you to **HCI (How Can I?)**, reminding you that it is important to always ask yourself a question instead of making a definitive statement. That encourages your mind to provide possibilities.

I speak to a lot of entrepreneurs as a business coach, and one of the things I hear them repeatedly say is… "I Can't." When you have already assigned a conclusion to the situation, there is no need for your mind to work on it. For that reason, "I Can't" is the most self-defeating thing you can say to yourself. It is essentially giving up before you even start.

- "I can't sell more than I did last year. I don't have any more time."
- "I can't beat the company recruiting record, I only have a few team members."

- "I can't earn an incentive trip. That is too hard, and I don't have the customer base."
- "I can't make my family support me. They will always think of me as the black sheep of the family."

We need to practice **HCI**…

"How Can I?"

- "**How can I** sell more than I did last year?"
- "**How can I** beat my personal best?"
- "**How can I** earn that incentive trip?"
- "**How can I** get my families' support?"

Remember, your brain automatically kicks into gear when you ask it a question. When you are a **Problem Solver** who rides the **Habit Train**, you will instinctively come up with three possible solutions for each question. Your brain is your own personal super computer; you just haven't been using it to its full potential.

Remember, your brainstorming can be anything from **Obvious to Outlandish**. It doesn't need to be realistic. Feel free to be creative!

"Give yourself the freedom to think, without putting up any roadblocks or barriers to your own creativity."

Let's look at the first **HCI** question above:

How can I sell more than I did last year?

- "I can clone myself."
- "I can hold multiple events at one time."
- "I can raise my prices."
- "I can sell more products to each person"
- "I can build a **Bundle** that includes products and services that have higher profit margins."
- "I can hire someone to sell for me."
- "I can create an online course once and sell it to everyone."

No idea is a "bad" idea when you are brainstorming. One of your outlandish ideas may be the catalyst to your next genius idea. In this case, a combination of these suggestions could create a virtual homerun that could send your sales into the stratosphere.

It is all about training yourself to think differently. You need to **Believe** you can find a solution. Let's talk about how **Dirty Filters** hinder your ability to find solutions, and then work on **Reframing.**

Dirty Filters

In **Chapter 3: The "F" Words**, we talked about **Filters** and how they affect the way we process information. We can have both positive and negative emotions about the same word, so context is important. If we have a **Dirty Filter**, (one that has been tainted by outside influences) we may gravitate toward the negative connotation instead of the positive.

When the mud, muck and mire cloud our **Filter**, it prevents us from being able to process information clearly. Without positive self-esteem continually clearing it away, we are stuck with a perpetually **Dirty Filter** and our view of the world becomes skewed.

A **Dirty Filter** is often the first cause of conflict with others, but using negatively charged words can be like adding a spark to a powder keg.

Power of Vocabulary

As I mentioned to you in **Chapter 9: Expert is NOT a Dirty Word**, Jim Rohn was my primary influence in recognizing the true power of vocabulary. I remember the following example he gave, because it illustrates the point so effectively.

When you are obviously in distress, which question would you prefer was posed to you?

Person A: What's WRONG with you?

Person B: What's TROUBLING you?

Person A could be perceived as judgmental. The word choice suggests that something is wrong **with** you. It implies that there is something that needs to be fixed, changed, or repaired.

Person B sounds concerned. They noticed you might be upset and they are interested in finding out more, so they can listen and assist you.

Although both questions may be used to uncover the source of the discomfort, one can sound harsh, judgmental or critical, even if that was not the intention. Carefully choosing your words can make a tremendous difference as you are connecting with people.

To be good at sales, recruiting, leadership or even relationships, you need to be good at communication. That means learning to articulate yourself well. You should try to extend **Grace** to others if their words seem inflammatory to you, recognizing that your own **Filter** affects how you feel.

When you find yourself on the receiving end of a conversation where you are interpreting someone's comments as negative, you need to **Believe** the best in others and **Reframe** the situation.

Reframing

Reframing is looking at the situation from a different perspective. That means actively seeking out an alternate explanation for someone else's actions, reactions or behaviors. In addition, it also involves finding alternative ways to view your own situation, challenges, and decisions. It involves a predilection for choosing the **Bright Side** and actively looking for positive options.

If your predisposition is to assume the negative, you need to condition yourself to look for the positive. Ask questions to understand the situation from the other person's perspective. You might be surprised by their answers and discover it was a miscommunication, often caused by a **Dirty Filter**. You may also become sympathetic or empathetic towards their circumstances by recognizing they too are influenced by their own **Filter**.

Giving Yourself Grace

Sometimes it is easier to give **Grace** to others, than it is to extend it to ourselves. When you make a mistake, are late, or are stuck in traffic, do you berate yourself?

Although I admittedly get frustrated, I make a mental note of what went wrong to cause the problem. Did I get up late, get distracted, take a short cut, etc. If it was a simple error, I move on. If it is a pattern that is causing the problem, I look for a solution to correct it for the future.

The point is, allowing the **Bully** to take hold of my feelings won't support my efforts. I choose to **Believe** that the diversion will create its own blessing or opportunity. It doesn't matter if that is true. Actively looking at the **Bright Side** is a CHOICE, and it keeps the negative emotions from taking over and derailing my efforts.

Here is an example where I could have been immobilized by a mistake, and instead chose to see it as an opportunity…

Finding the Bright Side

When I was scheduled to go to a hotel for a few days and finish this book, I couldn't find the manuscript on my computer or the servers. I scoured the drives and started to panic that I'd lost all my work. I started feeling completely overwhelmed and slipped into that **Bully Behavior** of beating myself up. The more I thought about it, the more stressed I became.

When we are overwhelmed, our hormones change. Cortisol is released into the body, and our thoughts become less focused and more easily distracted by outside influences. The **Bully** in your head loves it when you lose your **Confidence**. He enjoys it when **Doubt** and **FEAR** take over.

It is just this type of circumstance, where **Reframing** and choosing the **Bright Side** can save the day.

How did I handle this major setback?

I stopped and **prayed** about where the file was, willing to **accept** if I found it or not. **Acceptance** is the key component here. When you expect a specific outcome, it can set you up for disappointment and frustration. That is especially true when you have no control over the result.

I **Reframed** the situation by believing that if I was supposed to find it, I would. Otherwise, I was meant to write something better, and the Lord would inspire it. If I chose to focus on what I didn't have, I would have stayed stuck. You must train yourself to work through this behavior, so the **Habit Train** will automatically initiate **#BrightSide** thinking.

I still felt flustered, upset, and even disappointed in myself over this unfortunate situation. The **Bully** wanted me to get stuck in the **Weeds of Wallowing**, but I learned how to change my "state".

Make Your Move

At the time, I had recently come back from the Tony Robbins UPW event in San Jose. I remembered a little trick he shared called "**Make Your Move**", a process to change your state of mind. For me, I chose a kind of forward punch, once, then one, two, three more times. (If you want to see me "Making My Move", go to **www.VickiFitch.com/DS101**.)

The physical act of moving your body in a specific sequence while focusing on changing your mindset will become part of your **Habit Train.** It will help you to get out of the negativity, so you can readdress the problem or concern with a fresh perspective.

Come up with your own move and think of it as a 3-Step Process when you get overwhelmed.

1. Think about the **Bright Side**—you can always find something if you try. (Just like being a **Problem Solver**, utilize the **Obvious to Outlandish** philosophy.)
2. **Reframe** the situation and find something positive to concentrate on. Choose to **Believe** the best in yourself and others.
3. **Make Your Move**—to change your state of mind. (In the original manuscript, I hadn't been to UPW, so I wouldn't have known how to "Make My Move" **#BrightSide**)

NOTE: Be bold and choose your move now! I'd love for you to send me a quick video on what your move is on **Social Media**. Tag me in the post and use the hashtag **#MadeMyMove** so I can celebrate with you! (For more on using **Social Media** to build your business & your brand, check out *DS 301*)

If I had chosen to wallow in my frustration or misfortune, I could have lost an entire five-day trip. Instead I chose to **#EvictTheBully**, look at the **#BrightSide**, and remember there is *Profit in the Pain*.

Update: I was not able to find the draft before I left. But, I did write over 20,000 words during that trip, despite what happened at "**Hotel Hell**". (I will tell you all about it in **Chapter 17: Crushing It in Customer Service**.) The content flowed even better than the original version and I was also able to blend in more recent experiences, which added dimension to this project.

I **Believe** it is much better than the original version. What you BELIEVE is your REALITY, so continue to **Believe** the BEST.

Recovery from Setbacks

Setbacks are going to happen on your way to **Success Island**. The way you handle them will determine whether you get swept out to the **Ocean of Overwhelm** or work your way on to **Stability Shore**. Without experiencing setbacks, we wouldn't be able to appreciate the true value of the success we achieve.

"Setbacks are the hurdles we must endure
to truly understand our Success in life."

I have experienced overwhelming setbacks on my journey, including death and divorce. Those experiences have made me stronger and provided me the opportunity to share what I've learned with you. This map of Fitchipelago is a culmination of my experiences and a way for me to deliver the ups and downs I went through in an **Edutaining** way. I will be introducing you to many places and people throughout our journey together, and right now I want to introduce you to FRANK.

FRANK

If you have been in this industry for any length of time, you probably know **FRANK**. You may love **FRANK**, hate **FRANK,** or you may be just plain tired of **FRANK** but don't give up on him because he is actually a very helpful and loyal friend. Let's talk about how we can USE **FRANK** and be effective.

Who is FRANK?

FRANK is an acronym for:

F—**Friends**
R—**Relatives**
A—**Acquaintances**
N—**Neighbors**
K—**Kids**

It is the list of potential people to share your new business with. Most Direct Sales companies have you start with compiling this list of people you know. This helps you think of people who might be interested in your new venture whether as a customer, a hostess, a team member, or as your support system.

When I do **NCT** (**New Consultant Training**), we use this list as a tool to transform your business. In *DS 201*, I provide a step-by-step process, including exercises to do for yourself and with your team. It isn't about calling everyone on the list. It is a simple process of understanding how the mind works and effectively opening it to the possibilities.

Since this book is called *Direct Selling 101*, I don't want to overwhelm you with too many details. For now, let's just do this simple exercise to help you create a list of people that you know.

If you have a sheet of paper, you can just list the letters of the word **FRANK** down the side of the page. If you are like me and prefer forms, go to **www. VickiFitch.com/DS101** and download your copy so you always have one handy.

Start by making a list of all your Friends, using the reminders below to make sure you aren't forgetting people you know. Repeat the process for each letter of the word **FRANK** and try to concentrate on each specific demographic.

F—Friends—Current friends, past friends, friends of friends

R—Relatives—Parents, grandparents, siblings, cousins, aunts, uncles, etc.

A—Acquaintances—People you have met casually but are memorable

N—Neighbors—Current neighbors, past neighbors, parents' neighbors, etc.

K—Kids—Neighborhood kids, local sports or dance teams, local pageants, etc.

Be careful here. Don't be legalistic on what category a person belongs in. It doesn't matter. It is simply a tool to help you start thinking about who you know.

One common objection I hear is that Kids are not the target market for certain companies. Your product or service may not have a primary function for children but that shouldn't stop you from recognizing that children are your future customers. In addition, if you can find a way to improve a child's health, attention, awareness, education, social skills, etc., you will connect with their parents.

"Kids are a conduit to their parents and when they think fondly of you, their parents will too."

In **DS 201**, I go into details on all the ways your product or service may be used as a **Market Separator**, including unique ways to assist integrating parents with their children at your events.

Now that you have met, and have hopefully become well acquainted with **FRANK,** you are probably wondering...

What do I do with FRANK?

It is said that the average person knows a minimum of 600 people. In general, most people can easily recall approximately 5% of those relationships. Therefore, your list should include around thirty people.

If not, check yourself. Did you exclude names of people you know because you predetermined they wouldn't be interested? Be careful not to prejudge. Don't worry, you don't have to call all these people; this is just a list.

Statistically, about 10% of those people will immediately support you in your business venture. Some will be based on interest and others will be based on your relationship. Either way is fine. You will "Wow" them with your knowledge, and they will fall in love with the products, services, and benefits like you did.

The next step is simple. Choose three people that you feel would support your new business from the lists you've created and circle them.

Yes, just three to start.

These first three people are the catalysts to building your business. Your goal is to schedule two to three additional events or presentations from each one you hold. These events will be where your next hostesses, customers, referral sources, and potential recruits will come from.

It doesn't matter if these are in-person demonstrations, on-line meetings, events, or trainings. Whatever type of presentations you do, just choose your top three candidates, so you have somewhere to start.

If you just moved to a new city or location, here are some suggestions to help you get started.

- If you are close enough, schedule something in your old neighborhood or go to visit your family or friends in that location.
- Hold a **Virtual Event** (Yes, you can hold a virtual event! *DS 301* has the answers!)
- **Stop n Shops** at work places. You can bring your products to their work place during lunch or a special break time.
- **Lunch n Learns**
- *DS 201* has a more extensive list that includes ideas for specialty and themed events as well!

So now that you have picked your first three names, what do you do next? Now, it is time to Schedule.

Chapter 11

THE ART OF BEING A SUPER SCHEDULER

"The bad news is, time flies.
The good news is, you're the pilot."
– Michael Altshuler

B efore we start scheduling, you need to make sure you have set up your calendar with the days that you are available to do events, meetings, etc. If you have done the **Rock Star Guide to Gettin' It Done**, you should have your open days for the next two to four weeks readily available. You will soon see that knowing when you are available is the first step to becoming a Super Scheduler.

If you started this chapter saying, "Vicki, we don't schedule events in my business. I don't need this chapter." I say, "Think again." You may not be scheduling an event in the traditional **Party Plan** industry, but you are likely going to want people to attend a convention, meeting, webinar, or introductory meet-up to help them get acquainted with your business. Therefore, understanding the best way to do that will serve you no matter what industry you are in.

In order to perfect your scheduling skills, we must first understand the **Pain Points** associated with the specific type of appointment you are trying to set. For this example, I am going to be scheduling a **Party Plan** type event because it has the most objections associated with it. This method can be easily modified for a different type of appointment.

Scheduling Pain Points

When we talk about scheduling **Pain Points**, they are usually based on the following concerns:

- Low/No Attendance
- Low/No Sales

We touched on this in **Chapter 5: Quit Your Fitchin'** when I shared my feeling about my first workshop. I logically understood that the attendance of my guests wasn't actually a measurement of my worth, but the feelings and the **FEAR** were still real.

Most people who coordinate events have a **FEAR** about people showing up. They will even get desperate enough to invite or sometimes beg people to attend. Inviting people just to fill seats is what I call **Warm Body Syndrome** and I address handling this issue in *DS 201*.

They may say things like…

"**I don't know enough people**."
"**No one will come**."
"**My friends don't have any money**."
"**My friends are all "partied" out and don't want to come to any more events**."

Take note, none of those statements were, "I don't like your products and my friends won't either." The **FEAR** is based on the outcome. They are worried you will judge them as being unsuccessful because their friends didn't show up, or because they didn't buy your products. To be a Super Scheduler, you must alleviate the stress from your potential hostesses and make it a pleasant experience.

These, like any other objections, can easily be worked through with kindness, consideration, and guidance. Here is a sample conversation that will help us address each of the issues above.

You: "Mary, you had such a great time tonight. I would love to help you earn some free products for yourself. Wouldn't it be fun if we had a group together for you to get some free or discounted products?"

Hostess Mary: "Of course, it would be great, but **I don't really know enough people.**"

You: "I understand where that can be a concern, but if you are willing to allow me to invite some guests as well, do you think between the two of us we might be able to gather a few people together to share something new? Even some of tonight's guests would probably love to come and find out more about *(insert new topic here)* In **DS 201,** I share ideas on how to create modified events that will have a customer coming back multiple times.

Hostess Mary: "That sounds great, but I know my **friends, and they are just "partied" out. What if they don't show up?**"

You: I will make this event simple and fun for you. All you need to do is provide me with the information to contact them, and I will do the rest. If you would help me by sharing your excitement, and perhaps sharing on **Social Media**, that will go a long way. And if it is just the two of us, you will have some private time with me to learn something special, and I can get to know you better. Does that sound **valuable** to you?"

Hostess Mary: "Even if we do get them to show up, they probably **won't spend any money**. It would be a waste of your time."

You: "How about you let me work on providing them an inspirational **Experience**, and if they aren't interested in what I have to offer, no problem. That is my job. I will just consider it practicing my presentation. So, let's pick a date that works for you and go from there."

That interaction comforted her concerns and gave her **Hope** that she isn't alone in the process. It also provided **Confidence** that she won't be judged for the outcome. We will take responsibility as long as she provides us with all the contact information we requested.

Now, it is time to move on to scheduling the actual date.

Picking and Sticking the Date

I have noticed that getting a committed date is a difficult area for some people to navigate. Your focus here is to help her choose a date that will work for both of your **Schedules**.

"A "Yes!" isn't a booking without a Date and a Time."

The typical consultant when she hears a "Yes" to booking, says,
"Great, when would you like to do it?"
The hostess will then say something like,
"Let me check with my friends and I will get back to you."
In Sales, we call that a **"Be Back"**. Regardless of whether it is about a sale or about scheduling an event, "I will get back to you." often means you won't hear back again. This doesn't mean they aren't interested. Life happens, and people get busy. Always schedule what you can immediately to avoid playing phone tag later.

Overcoming her objections, and her overwhelm, of the next 365 days of the calendar requires narrowing the options to help her decide. There are three main questions to ask.

Picking up where we left off in the conversation.

You: "So, let's pick a date that works for you and go from there. Would you like a Weekday or a Weekend?"

Hostess Mary: "Weekend."

You: "Perfect! Do you consider Friday night a Weekday or Weekend?"

Hostess Mary: "Weekend."

You: "Excellent! My first opening is next Friday at 7pm. How does that sound?"

Can you see what we did here? We took 365 days and condensed them into manageable pieces of information. She can look at her calendar and confirm, or choose another date.

When you pose a question with limitless possibilities, it can be overwhelming to think about in the moment. When you lead the discussion, you can offer her the dates that match both of your **Schedules**. (Check out the DOTS system in **DS 201** for more details on this process.)

As we continue with the conversation, you may come up with some additional objections, so let's address those as well.

Hostess Mary: "Well, that sounds good to me, but **I really need to ask my friends first** to make sure they will come."

You: "Mary, I understand why you want to do that. But if your friends are anything like mine, if I asked ten people what would work for them, I would likely get ten different answers. I recommend we pick the time that works best for YOU, and if we need to adjust it, we can. So, how about we do next Friday at 7pm since we know that works for both of us? This way, if any of the other ladies here want to attend, I can give them the details right now. We can always have a second event for those who can't make it and you can earn more rewards!"

In that brief conversation, we:

- Addressed her **FEAR**
- Offered a solution
- Provided urgency for choosing a date
- Inspired her to think about having multiple events (Premiere Hostess **DS 201**)

If she still feels hesitant about the date, continue offering the next available dates, until you find one that works for both of you.

The Extra Mile

We have already determined that since she is here, if we can get everything we need, that is the ideal situation. Have your hostess packets made up in advance and be prepared with a small gift if she provides the information requested right now. (If you are brand new to this industry, your company usually has small or inexpensive items used to reward people for helping you build your business. Ask your **Upline** or company representative what the company offers and what they recommend. In *DS 201*, I give suggestions for many industries on what you can use for **Market Separators** and giveaways!)

Let's continue with the conversation.

You: "I'm so excited to do this event for you, Mary. I want it to be fun and fabulous for you and your friends, so here is your hostess packet. It reviews the basics of what you already know and outlines some additional opportunities for you to earn additional gifts.

1. *Getting me your guest list today*
2. *Keeping your originally scheduled date*
3. *Getting (3) Outside orders/bookings*

I want to make things incredibly easy for you, so if you can provide me with your guest list tonight, I have a free gift for you. Many of your guests are already in your phone, so just share their information on this sheet. I will take care of the rest."

For those of you who are tech savvy, have them share the vCard or VCF file from their phones. We can then send out **T-Vites** to make it fast and easy! If you aren't ready to utilize the benefits of **High Tech**, no problem! The standard invitation strategies are a great start.

Show her a sample of the invites you will send out, so she knows what her friends will be receiving, and continue with your conversation.

You: "There is a guest list included in your hostess packet for anyone else that you want to invite who isn't in your phone. I will get all the invitations out for you and follow up with your guests as well."

NOTE: Social Media is a great tool to help get the word out. But it should be an added layer of support, not your primary tool, if you want to set yourself apart. I will review this thoroughly in *DS 301*.

What is a T-Vite

If case you are unfamiliar, a **T-Vite** is a Text Invitation. We can send them out via email or text, and even print and send them in the mail if necessary. They are visually appealing and provide all the details of the event in one simple step. Once you have created the template, you can change the name, date, time, and location for each new event, in seconds.

In *DS 201*, I have provided **T-Vite** Samples. In *DS 501*, I have outlined a completely automated follow up system that includes the sequence and strategy to secure long-term clients.

Step Up and Stand Out!

I know some of you have been taught, or told, that this business is easy because the hostess does all the work. You hand her the invites or create a **T-Vite** and the rest is up to her. If you have tried this method, you know that on an average, it works less than 50% of the time. (More like 10% of the time for most.) When the hostess is required to do the work, your results will usually suffer. Her business, job, family, etc. are going to come before this event. If her life gets busy, the first thing she usually skips is something that is going to require extra time and energy.

If you know people who are complaining about cancellations, they are probably having the hostess do the work. Calling the day before to see how many guests are coming is a poor strategy for long term growth. It will probably leave you feeling frustrated and defeated.

I know this next part isn't going to be popular with some of you, but you are reading this book because you wanted a guide to **#RockThatDream Ridge,** so I am going to give it to you straight. If you want this business to be successful, YOU need to do the work. For those of you who have experienced super success with letting your hostess do all the work…

NEWSFLASH!
"If your hostess does all the work for a successful event… she is a consultant that just isn't getting paid to do the job."

This is actually a good thing! **#BrightSide** you already have your first potential recruit! I will help you with that in **Chapter 14: Rock Star Recruiting.**

If you want to increase your sales, scheduling, and recruiting, do your job and let your hostess get excited about the products. It's great if she wants to follow up with her friends too, but don't leave that up to her. You are the best qualified person to get people excited about attending your events.

Another **Market Separator** for me was my style of doing pre-class calls. I personally contacted everyone who was invited. I sold product, booked events, and recruited consultants I had never even met before based on the secret I am sharing with you here.

The Difference Maker

After the invitations go out, you want to follow up with a personal phone call to each person. I know this is crazy to some of you, because you only use the phone to text or message, but check out my reasoning and see if you agree.

This is a sample follow up call after the invitations were sent. I would ask each person three pertinent questions based on the product or service I was providing. For example, in the jewelry industry, I wanted to be prepared in advance for people purchasing products. Therefore, I created some excitement, created some urgency, and set the expectation of their attendance.

Me: "Hi Jane, this is Vicki Fitch with XYZ Jewelry Company and I am doing the event for Mary this Friday night. How are you today?"

Jewelry Loving Jane: "Great, thank you."

Me: "I was just calling to see if you got the invitation we sent you, and to see if you are going to be able to make it?"

Jewelry Loving Jane: "I think so, I haven't checked my schedule yet."

Me: "No problem, I just have 3 quick questions for you. Why don't I ask you now so if you can make it, I will be prepared for you? Do you have a minute?"

Jewelry Loving Jane: "Sure."

Me: "First, what is your favorite color?"

Jewelry Loving Jane: "My favorite color is definitely red."

Me: "Great, I will make a note of that. What color clothes do you typically find yourself wearing?"

Jewelry Loving Jane: "I find myself wearing a lot of black, white, and brown. Oh my, I'm kind of boring, aren't I?"

Me: "Not at all! Those are great base colors that are actually very flexible for coordinating accessories. Do you have any outfits you have difficulty accessorizing or any special occasions coming up?"

Jewelry Loving Jane: "Oh my goodness, I forgot about the high school reunion next month. I also have a wedding to go to."

Me: "If you've already picked out the clothes you are going to wear to those events, do me a favor, and bring them with you. Try to come a few minutes early so I can match up the perfect pieces for you."

Jewelry Loving Jane: "Fantastic! I will do that!"

Me: "Remember, the event is on Friday night at 7pm at Mary's house. The address is on the invitation, and I am having an "On-Time Drawing." I recommend you come around 6:45pm so you can get in on that, and so I can help you look amazing for those events!"

Jewelry Loving Jane: "Can't wait! I will see you then!"

Me: "By the way, feel free to bring a friend or two with you, and I will reward you with a free gift for each one that attends. I recommend you have them call me or send me their information, so I can ask them the same questions and will be prepared for them too."

Jewelry Loving Jane: "Oh my gosh, I should bring Cece from work. She is going to the wedding too!"

Me: "Feel free to forward her information to me if you want me to contact her. Or forward her the **T-Vite** and ask her to call me if she can make it. I will see you on Friday at 6:45pm!"

That conversation is actually very similar to the ones I've experienced on a regular basis. People get invited to events all the time. Your goal is to get them excited enough that they commit to attending yours, and to inviting their friends.

Typically, if we get an invitation, we make a mental note about the event but don't necessarily mark it on the calendar. Without a reminder and no real excitement, we are less likely to attend. We may simply forget or allow anything else that comes up to be an easy distraction. If someone suggests we go grab a bite to eat, we may choose that option because there is a personal connection. **Human to Human (#H2H)** contact is a powerful draw.

Making it Personal

What makes this invitation different is that our initial phone call starts to form a relationship. Your potential guest will get off the phone and immediately go to their closet. They will choose their outfits for those two events and set them aside. We have actively engaged a different part of the brain, and now have excitement and commitment on our side.

We all want to look good at the events we attend, especially weddings and reunions. Now, with the couple of extra minutes you invested, your guests will be anticipating meeting you, and are already interested in what you have to offer.

You brilliantly used the **WIIFM** method. They are no longer attending just to support a friend… there is something in it for them! A personal stylist is going to help them accessorize.

This simple process of connecting with people personally before the event is a game changer. When it is done consistently, it will result in higher attendance, more bookings, and larger sales at every event.

Now that your guest is excited to attend, when Friday rolls around and someone asks her if she wants to grab something to eat, she will be more likely to say something like…

Jewelry Loving Jane: "Sure, as long as we can be done by 6:15pm. I have to be at Mary's at 6:45pm. You should come with me. A professional stylist is going to help us put together some stunning accessories."

People crave connection. So many people use technology as their only means of communication, but the touch of a hug, the gleam of a smile, the inflection of someone's voice, and the look in their eyes creates a relationship. When you add the interaction of other guests, it becomes an **Experience** which everyone will want to recreate.

One of the guests on my podcast, **Vicki Fitch Live: A Fresh Perspective,** was best-selling author, Bryan Kramer. He did a TED Talk on **#H2H**. (There is a link to this presentation **www.VickiFitch.com/DS101**) His premise is,

---

"We don't do business B2B or B2C
(Business to Business or Business to Consumer),
we do business H2H (Human to Human),
and that connection will supersede
so many of the other things in our lives".
– Bryan Kramer

Relationships are what make our lives more fulfilling. We enjoy purchasing products from people who care about us because it makes us feel valued and appreciated. Set yourself apart from the other representatives out there who are trying to make a living **off** other people. Instead, **stand out** as someone who makes a living **helping** other people.

Implementing these simple strategies will fill your events with excited participants and keep your calendar full. Now it is time to teach you my philosophy on selling, and how it will change the way you do business forever.

Chapter 12
HOW TO BE A STELLAR SELLER

"Sales Success is 80% Attitude and only 20% Aptitude."
– Brian Tracy

I t is imperative as an entrepreneur that you know how to successfully navigate **Sales Street** because it is one of the main thoroughfares on **Success Island**. Many people are challenged with the idea that they are in "Sales" and try to divert their travel to **Barter Blvd** to avoid the potential difficulty of asking for money. It is my hope by the end of this series, that you travel proudly down **Sales Street** and that you teach your team to follow your lead.

There is a stigma some have attached to the title "salesperson", which is not only outdated, but unwarranted. Granted, there are people in any industry that give their profession a bad name, but it is time to accept that stereotype isn't you. It is time we **Reframe** the situation, so you can see that selling is an important part of any business. There is a need for honest people to help others find products and services that are truly beneficial. It's time for you to step up and I want to show you how.

Definition of Sales

I know many of you are tempted to close this book and say, "I am not a salesperson!"

I get it. You have heard of or experienced someone in sales that was out for themselves, and now you are afraid to be mistaken for that kind of person. Most people experience **FEAR** regarding sales because they don't want to be judged or rejected, and they don't want to be labeled "pushy".

The first place to start is my definition of Sales:

---

*"Sales is simply providing enough information
for people to make an informed decision."*

Think about how freeing that is. Your job is not to "sell" the product. It is to provide enough information, including your **Expert** opinion, to help others understand how your offering will improve their lives.

Your job is to find a way to solve their problems with your products and services. Sometimes, that means having to identify **Pain Points** that they didn't even know existed.

Introducing a Pain Point

At a networking event in my area one evening, I was introduced to a **Pain Point** I wasn't aware of. The speaker was from LegalShield, a Direct Sales company that levels the legal playing field by providing unlimited legal services for a small monthly fee. She started by asking the group some general questions like:

- Have you ever gotten a traffic ticket?
- Have you ever been overcharged for a repair or paid an unfair bill?
- Have you ever signed a contract?
- Have you gotten your Will or Health Care Directive done?

This last question was the one that got my attention because there was a story attached to it that became relevant to me.

"Do any of you have adult children?"

She paused as she waited for the crowd to raise their hands.

"Did you know that without a Health Care Directive on file, if something happens to them, and they are unable to speak for themselves, you would have NO RIGHTS to direct their care?"

That question stung me like I had just been slapped in the face. We live in California, and at the time, our 19-year-old son was attending college in Chicago, Illinois. Thinking about the possibility that something could happen to him, and I would have no legal rights to make decisions on his behalf, was incredibly sobering.

Can you imagine how you would feel if your son or daughter was incapacitated by a critical car accident, and you had no rights to tell the medical staff what your child would or would not want done? To be honest, the thought was a bit overwhelming.

When I became aware of the **Pain Point**, I immediately wanted a solution. Since LegalShield was the answer, it made for a very easy sale. After recognizing the value it provided, my husband and I agreed it was the perfect fit for his clients as an additional service in his practice. He has since retired from his financial services business and is an Executive Director with LegalShield. Our oldest son, who has now graduated from college, is already a Director, and the two of them are working the business together.

Introducing a **Pain Point,** to your target market can create a ripple effect. The speaker gave me **enough information to make an informed decision,** I shared it with my husband, and the bonus was, she got a top leader on her team by doing it. That being said, there is some skill involved in providing "enough information" without going overboard. It is also important to organize the information in a way that makes sense to your customers. The best way to do that is by asking **relevant** questions.

Ask Relevant Questions

There is a difference between asking questions that will help you provide great service and participating in an inquisition. The **FEAR** that if you ask too many questions your customer may be offended, frustrated or not want to do business with you, may prevent you from being successful.

The truth is the complete opposite. If you are asking questions that are **relevant** to the client's needs, they will be highly engaged in the conversation.

I Don't Want to be Salesy, Sleazy or Cheesy

We all know the unfortunate stereotype of a "Used Car Salesman". It is one of **Salesy, Sleazy and Cheesy** gimmicks, or attempts to be sly. The **FEAR** that they will pressure you, or sell you something you don't want, is what plagues most people. No one wants to get taken advantage of.

The truth is, used cars can be a great value. When a representative asks questions that are **relevant** to the purchase, it shows they are in tune with your family's needs. Capitalizing on their trusted expertise is what creates repeat customers and **Raving Fans**.

Think about it. If you are shopping for a car and the salesperson asks you questions about your family size, transportation needs, and your audio and entertainment preferences, are you offended or appreciative?

What if they make recommendations based on the information they gathered that would help your family? For instance, if your salesperson said,

"With multiple children, you may want to consider the entertainment upgrade, which includes USB charging stations for every seat."

Even if they were recommending you purchase a newer model or a more expensive vehicle, when someone understands a potential **Pain Point,** and helps you resolve it in advance, that creates a positive impression.

It is the representative's job to offer you the options, it is your job to decide what you want.

Now let's go back to talking about your business. When your recommendations are focused on your clients' needs, they will trust your guidance. In turn, you need to understand **Buying Thresholds**, and how they can affect your sales.

What is a Buying Threshold?

"A Buying Threshold is an imaginary number that a person won't spend on themselves, without either feeling guilty or consulting another person about their purchase."

Consulting other people doesn't mean they can't make their own decisions. They may have an obligation (to a spouse or significant other), or perhaps they are just looking for some moral support to justify their decisions. Our **Filters** create these circumstances and we need to treat them with respect.

We all have a **Buying Threshold** and once we have reached it, most Direct Sales people stop selling to the customer. It is almost a subconscious assumption that the customer is done shopping. I want you to understand this is a disservice to your clients, because their wants and needs are different from yours.

The most important phrase I could share with you to serve your customers better is this…

"Don't Stop Selling until your
CUSTOMER
is done buying."

Notice that the word **CUSTOMER** is in all caps and underlined. That is because it is the key word in the sentence. Sales should always be about the **CUSTOMER**. Not about you, your **Buying Threshold**, your commission, or anything else. It is all about your **CUSTOMER**.

In my opinion, analogies are one of the best and easiest ways to convey a point. Let's imagine for a moment…

You just received an invitation for a very prestigious Black-Tie Gala...

All the influential people you've been wanting to meet will be there, and you want to dress to impress. It is time to go shopping.

You shop for hours or days, hunting through dozens of stores, looking for the perfect dress. After what often feels like an eternity, you finally find it. It fits perfectly in all the right places and you look amazing! You are confident, heads will be turning, and people will remember you.

*You head home, excited about your purchase while thinking about the double take glances that will be happening at the event. When you arrive, you can't wait to show everyone at home your incredible find. It will be fun to hear a little positive reinforcement about how fantastic you look in that dress! You run to your room, put it on, and suddenly your moment of **Confidence** quickly turns the corner to **Doubt**.*

Your shoes don't match, your accessories are completely out of style, and you have no jewelry to go with your new outfit. Your excited high, suddenly turns into a disappointed low. And, it could have been prevented... with the right questions.

So, now in this disillusioned state, do you go all the way back to the store you finally found your dress in, or do you go to the closest place to get the job done?

If you are like most of us, you're busy, so you will typically go to the closest place to where you are. We want that euphoric feeling back as soon as possible, so we can feel good about our choices and reclaim the excitement about the event we will be attending.

Since most places that sell evening wear sell accessories to complete their ensembles, we are going to assume that the store where this dress was purchased did as well. By not providing all the options available, the salesperson did a disservice...

- To the customer, because they have to go shopping again to find what else they need.

- To the store, because the customer will buy the accessories from their competitor.
- To themselves, if they are on commission, because they lost the additional sales.

So WHY did this happen? It could have been due to laziness, busyness, lack of skill, or absence of training. However, the most common reason salespeople don't offer the customer all the available options is **FEAR**.

- **FEAR** that the customer will label them as "pushy".
- **FEAR** that the customer will say "No" and reject their ideas, suggestions, or even worse, them personally.
- **FEAR** of making a mistake or not knowing what to do.

FEAR prevents people from growing. We hide it, we disguise it, and we pretend it isn't there. We even make excuses for why we do it, when in reality, we should embrace the **SKILL of Asking Questions** and do our JOB.

Nordstrom Service

Whether you love Nordstrom or not, the one thing they are known for worldwide is customer service. My favorite way to shop is through their Personal Shopping Service. As a matter of fact, it is what I modeled my Direct Sales business on. I have provided an in-depth look at the process of how to triple your sales by using this simple model in *DS 201* (Read the chapter called **The Power of the PSA**).

So, let's revisit this scenario again.

You just received an invitation for a very prestigious Black-Tie Gala…

You call your Personal Shopper at Nordstrom, share the details about the occasion, and schedule an appointment.

When you arrive, Nancy at Nordstrom has elegantly displayed the selections she chose for the occasion in a large dressing room. On one side of the full-length mirror, there are dual hanging racks, while the other side is lined up with shoes and accessories to match the couture. There is a chilled bottle of water waiting for you next to a comfortable chair, and your personal stylist greets you with a smile!

Before I go on with the story, how are you feeling right now? Can you see the clothes and the shoes that are pre-selected in your size, waiting for you to try them on?

Before the **Bully in your Head** starts telling you that you can't afford Nordstrom, allow me to start by telling you the service is FREE—no charge to you whatsoever. You have no obligation to buy, and you can provide your budget before going in. Do they want you to buy more? Of course, they are a retail store. But, the service is designed to help you relax while you shop.

An **Expert** stylist has been tasked with finding the items, so you know they will coordinate well. No need to go find a different size dress, Nancy will do it for you. Need a slip or different bra? Nancy will be right back. You get to spend your time trying things on and deciding which options are right for you. They provide this service to keep you coming back over and over again. Nordstrom recognizes your lifetime value as a customer.

You try on the outfits and have narrowed it down to a couple choices. Nancy gives you her professional opinion, because it is her JOB. She then has you try on the accessories with your final choice.

You look beautiful, but Nancy says, "Wait, let me show you one more thing that will make you look even more SPECTACULAR!"

Do you say…

"NO! Don't you dare try to help me look better! Keep your ideas to yourself and leave me alone!"

Of course not. You want to see the full ensemble, the complete package, the icing on the cake…

You want to know your OPTIONS.

Nancy isn't pressuring you to buy everything. Her JOB is to SHOW you everything. It is your job to choose what you want to take with you.

Do you see the point here?

Nancy has pampered you and cared for you, probably for several hours. You have gotten to **KNOW** her and have bonded during this process. You **LIKE** her, and she has become a trusted advisor during your time here. You **TRUST** her opinions, because when an outfit didn't suit your body type or style, she told you there was a better fit among your selections. That is the **Trifecta**. The **Know, Like, & Trust Factor** (**KLT**) that makes you WANT to buy from her.

Does that feel **Salesy, Sleazy or Cheesy**? No, it feels natural, helpful, and fun. That is the experience we want to provide our customers to keep them coming back to us again and again.

Now that we have discussed Nordstrom Service, let's go back to you, and the things holding you back from doing what Nancy just did.

Are you Blocking Their Buying?

As we take a moment to look at your specific business, it is important to address your **Buying Threshold** and how you may be blocking their buying, without realizing you are doing it.

For a moment, try to think about your own **Buying Threshold**. Ask yourself these questions:

1. How much money are you comfortable spending on yourself without feeling guilty, or consulting someone else?
2. How much is your average sale per person?
3. Are the numbers for item #1 and item #2 similar?
4. Have you been uncomfortable about telling a customer the total of their bill?
5. Have you ever gotten nervous about offering another product or service, because you thought it might go over their budget?

If you answered "Yes" to any of those questions, you were probably passed your own **Buying Threshold,** so it is important you remember…

"It is YOUR JOB
to offer up all the solutions.
It is THEIR JOB
to make the decision on what they want to purchase.
It is not your place to put people on a budget. "

You should always recommend what you **Believe** is in the best interests of your CUSTOMER. Your recommendations shouldn't change, unless the data you are working with changes.

You may recognize you have been guilty of pre-judging people and their discretionary income in the past. It is nothing to be ashamed of; it is just something you need to consciously adjust for the future. Your JOB is to serve others. You need to care enough about them to show them everything that is available to meet their needs. Then, let them make their own decisions.

Sometimes, our **Filter** can cloud our ability to relate to concepts that have monetary values attached, so I want you to answer the questions below.

Your very best friend in the world just came to your house. She is going somewhere incredibly special and needs the perfect dress that makes her look and feel beautiful.

What do you do?
- *Grab any old dress that might fit,* **OR**
- *Go to your best dresses and see which is the most flattering on her?*

- *Send her home with just a dress and assume she has accessories at home,* **OR**
- *Pull out your shoes and handbags that match the dress and let her choose?*

- *Send her home to figure out jewelry on her own,* **OR**
- *Pull out your jewelry and see what looks best on her?*

The more important question is… do you see my point? The principle is still the same, we only removed the money from the equation. A good friend would show her the best she had to offer and allow her to make her own choices?

As a friend… our JOB is to offer our best suggestions and honest opinions.

As a salesperson… our JOB is to offer the best suggestions and honest opinions.

"Selling is like Friendship.
It is all about caring for your clients
and offering them the best you have available."

Understanding your audience and what is best for them is a critical part of building relationships. The best way to do that is to develop the **SKILL of Asking Questions.**

Chapter 13

THE SKILL OF ASKING QUESTIONS

"Asking the right questions takes as much skill
as giving the right answers."
– Robert Half

avigating your way to **Success Island** takes time and **SKILL**. It isn't just looking at the map. It is **asking** relevant questions about the best way to get there. It is **listening** to others who have already been there to prevent the pitfalls that you can't see. It is **learning** new options and finding others to accompany you on the trip. Anyone can ask "Where is **Success Island**?" but what you really want to know is how to get to **#RockThatDream Ridge**.

You saw from our trip on **Hope Helo** that the terrain can be tricky, so the emphasis in this chapter is **SKILL**. I want to help you become an effective communicator and a creative connector through the **SKILL** of asking questions. The relationships you make along the way will help you trust the terrain, so you can confidently lead the way for those that follow you.

The Art of Asking

As you know from the last chapter, there is a difference between asking relevant questions and participating in an inquisition. Have you ever been around someone who asked you a million questions? (Okay, so I know they didn't literally ask you a million, but sometimes the rapid-fire delivery system, or the unrelated nature of the questions that were asked, caused you to pause…)

When we are genuinely interested in people and the answers they give, people feel the vibe, and it creates a unique connection. When you actually care about a person, their profession, their family, or their hobbies, it can create an instant "bridge" that leads to a relationship. Those relationships help us develop **Raving Fans**, instead of the "one-off" or what we call the "**One & Done**" sale. It is also the gateway to referrals and repeat business. Let's dive a little deeper into what the **SKILL** of asking questions means.

The definition of the word **SKILL**:

Skill—the ability to do something well; expertise.

Your mission, should you choose to accept it, is to develop the expertise to ask people GREAT questions. Not good questions or adequate questions, but GREAT questions. Questions that make people think, feel, and respond. Questions that show you are listening and that you care about what others think and say.

In order to do this well, you need to look for things you have in common. This way, you can contribute to the conversation and add **value**. Make sure not to use it as a bumper guard to bounce the conversation back to you, so you can jump in and dominate it at the first possible chance.

People generally like to talk about themselves, so although you may have no trouble getting people to open up, you need to find your common ground to allow the relationship to grow.

TMI Syndrome

There are people who are prone to oversharing or what I call "**Gushing**". This is a symptom of a deeper concern called **TMI Syndrome** (translation: **Too Much**

Information Syndrome). I speak more on this in *DS 201*, so you can effectively learn to contribute to these conversations and lead them back to a place of connection.

Before we go on discussing the **SKIILL** of asking questions, let's do a little quiz to see if you are suffering from **TMI Syndrome**: (This could be a little painful for some of you, but be honest about your answers so we can get you on track to be a **Rock Star!**)

TMI Syndrome Quiz

1. When someone asks what you do, do you take a deep breath and launch into your 30 second commercial and then keep going with the features and benefits of your products and services?
2. Do you find yourself being ready to "jump in" to the conversation when someone else is speaking, thinking of what you are going to say next, instead of listening to everything they are saying?
3. Do you share personal details about your life, medical conditions, problems, and relationship challenges when you meet someone for the first time?
4. Do you ever feel like people are avoiding you or are looking for an opportunity to get away from you at social events?
5. When people are sharing with you, are you thinking about what you could sell them or why they need your product or service?

If you answered yes to 1 question, you are showing **Signs** of **TMI Syndrome**. I recommend inoculation by reading this chapter multiple times and practicing the **BYT "Bite Your Tongue"** method. (I know it sounds like you are punishing yourself but read **Chapter 14: Rock Star Recruiting** and you'll understand why.)

If you answered yes to 2 questions, you are still in the **Early Stages.** Most people haven't noticed or been infected by it yet, so we need to get it under control as soon as possible. There are some that are acutely aware, so you may have some work to do proving that you are cured.

If you answered yes to 3 questions, you are at the **Need Intervention Stage**. Most of the world recognizes that you have **TMI Syndrome**, but only a few brave souls are willing to bring it to your attention. You've been angry at these people in the past and may have mistaken them for **Naysayers**, when they really were just trying to help you "Keep it real."

If you answered yes to 4 questions, you have a **Serious Case** of **TMI Syndrome**. It is affecting your business and your personal life. You probably feel a bit isolated and frustrated that people don't seem to truly connect with you. Those that do connect tend to withdraw, which upsets you. An immediate intervention is necessary. You need to go on full lock down mode and commit to asking questions and **learning** about others. When asked what you do, you can give them a maximum ten-word answer, which is immediately followed by, "So tell me more about what you do." **Cold Turkey** is the only remedy for you. Don't fool yourself and think you can take a dip back in the water until you have professional assistance!

If you answered yes to all 5 questions. You have reached the critical **Need Executive Coaching Stage**! Do not pass go, do not collect $200! You must go right to the Executive Coaching infirmary, where we will practice the **SKILL** of asking questions until we have cured you of **TMI Syndrome**. Never fear! We will prevail!

Obviously, I am being a little facetious here, but chances are you know exactly what I am talking about.

The **TMI Syndrome** may have been brought on by you being nervous so you found yourself oversharing. Or maybe a well-intentioned **Upline** told you to get out there and tell people what you do. Whatever it was, you are now aware that it is probably prohibiting you from creating deeper relationships with people. You now know that you need to concentrate on **listening** and **learning** about others.

Focus on the fact that becoming the best version of yourself is really what we are after. Moreover, really getting to know people and knowing how you can serve their needs are important parts of business that really can't be replaced.

Hopefully, I have scared you out of **TMI Syndrome**. That quiz was designed to be your inoculation. When you see it spelled out and are faced with the damage that can be done, it tends to get you back on track. (I call that a **#FitchTap**. It provides a **Nudge** to get you back on course, without requiring the full strength of the **#Fitchslap**) Let's wrap this back around to the **SKILL** of asking questions.

Build Relationships

Let me preface what I am about to discuss by saying, I am an entrepreneur. Being an entrepreneur means I want to monetize what I do and how I spend my time. So, having a plan and wanting to share my business is natural. It is the end result we are looking for. BUT, your main objective should be to **BUILD RELATIONSHIPS FIRST!**

If your product or service is a good fit for the person you are speaking to, understanding more about them will be a positive catalyst in the relationship, and even the selling process. I am bringing this up because I've seen other books and heard other people say, "Don't tell them what you do," "Keep the mystery," or "Keep them guessing." In my opinion, that is RIDICULOUS.

Let me say it again. I think that is RIDICULOUS! If that was their attempt at curing you of **TMI Syndrome**, it is a lousy remedy. If they think it is somehow cool to keep people guessing, they are dealing with the wrong type of people. What I mean by that is most self-respecting people want to develop real relationships and purchase products from people they **Know, Like, & Trust (KLT)**.

If you avoid my questions about what you do, it doesn't make me want to dive deeper and find out more about you. It tells me that you are either new in your industry, insecure about your business, or have gotten some coaching from someone who is targeting individuals that respond to manipulative techniques. None of these things are a good fit for me as an entrepreneur, or as a person.

I also want to point out that I have no problem working with someone who is new in their industry. If they can deliver what I need, when I need it, we are a good fit. If they are seeking how to be the best they can and are willing to find the answers, I say more power to them. We all had to start out somewhere, and if I can support your journey, I am honored to do so where it is appropriate. If I have to do the research on what is best for me in order to purchase from you, that is a deal breaker. I don't have the time, nor the interest, in doing your job for you. But, I do love to support entrepreneurs who are rocking it in their space.

Networking

Networking events are one of the easiest places to watch **Gushing** and the **SKILL of Asking Questions** in the same room. Let's watch this scene at a networking event where we have a new person and a seasoned veteran meeting each other for the first time.

> **Carrie:** "Hi! I'm Coach Carrie, what do *you* do?"
>
> Helen is at her first networking meeting. She is thrilled that someone singled her out and has taken an interest in her and her business.
>
> Helen proceeds to answer.
>
> **Helen:** "I am Helpful Helen, and I have a technical resources company."

Now that we have set the scene, let me share examples of the right way and wrong way to connect with the prospect.

WRONG:

Carrie: (answering with the speed of a hummingbird) "That is great! I am a networking coach who teaches entrepreneurs how to make meaningful connections at events like this. You should come to my workshop next Friday evening. It would really help you build your connections. Are you available? (without a pause for an answer, she proceeds)

You could improve your business by building relationships with other people in the community. I have a lot of connections here and can introduce you to others who might be able to assist you. Do you have a card? Here is mine. I will send you the details of the event. It was nice meeting you!"

Helen: (stands there dumbfounded) She still hasn't said anything, and Carrie handed her a card and walked off. Helen feels confused because she initially thought Carrie had an interest in her business. She is now feeling a bit discouraged. The more frequently this happens, the more she may become jaded about networking events. Falsely assuming that no one really cares about what she does anyway, eventually she may either change her style to that of Carrie, so she can feel "heard", or she will continue to be a wallflower and assume that this is just the way networking goes.

BETTER:

Carrie: "Hi! I'm Coach Carrie. What do you do?"

Helen: "I am Helpful Helen, and I have a technical resources company."

Carrie: "How fabulous! Technology is such an important part of business today! What area of technology do you specialize in?"

Helen: "I help small businesses understand how to use the technology that is available to them by making it less confusing."

Carrie: "Do you help with certain programs or are you a full resource company?"

Helen: "I'm sorry it is taking me so long to tell you what I do. I am struggling with how to say it. My company is composed of people in many areas of technology, and our goal is to be the place people go to when they are confused with their technology. We want to help them make sense of it all."

Carrie: "I see! That is amazing! I can honestly say I could use your services! Do you have a card?"

Helen: "Of course! Here it is." (Remember, Helen is new. She may not know to ask about your business, so here is an easy transition for this conversation.)

Carrie: "I am so glad we met, Helen! You shared that you were having difficulty expressing what you do in a quick and easy way. As a networking coach, I help people with that all the time. May I offer a suggestion that might help you feel more confident in your sharing?"

Helen: "Of course! I would love that!"

Carrie: "How about something like this, "I am Helpful Helen, and I have a technical resources company that helps entrepreneurs easily 'tackle their tech'." That reply is fast and simple. It also gives people plenty of opportunity to ask questions about your business, which might lead into a detailed conversation about the specifics of how you could assist them.

Helen: "WOW! That is perfect. Thank you so much for your help!"

Carrie: "It is my pleasure, Helen! I'd also love to invite you to an event I am having next week. I can introduce you to some people whom I think might be a good fit for your company. Perhaps we could also talk a bit more about how I can utilize your services."

Helen: "That would be wonderful! Thank you for the invitation!"

Carrie: "Here is my card. I will follow up with you via email with all the details and reminders, because we can all use the help of technology! I look forward to connecting next week!"

I obviously realize that since I wrote that "script", it was an easy transition. Not all conversations are like that, but more of them could be if you **learned** to **listen** and **ask** the right questions. In the preceding conversation with Helen and Carrie, note that we took one talking point with meaningful answers, and built a bridge to future conversations.

Things you should take note of:

1. Everything in the second conversation was **AUTHENTIC.**
2. Carrie was more **FOCUSED** on finding out about Helen and what she did, than figuring out a way to sell her something or have her attend an event.
3. Carrie found a way to **RELATE** to Helen's business.
4. Carrie asked for **PERMISSION** to offer Helen a suggestion or solution.
5. Carrie offered **VALUE** to Helen with no **Expectation** of something in return.
6. Carrie was able to **BLEND** in what she did to the conversation.
7. Carrie set **FOLLOW UP** into the conversation. Helen knows an invite is coming and is expecting to reconnect.

Deeper Dive

Did you notice the questions were peppered in between meaningful answers? If you want to build relationships, focus on questions that help you understand people and how you can help them. If you are wondering how to utilize that skill in the areas of Sales, Scheduling and Recruiting, the philosophy is the same— Connect and Care. Below are some questions to blend into your conversations to create engagement.

1. What are the biggest challenges in your industry or for your customers?
2. What things do you **Believe** set you apart from your competition?
3. If you had a magic wand, what three things would you change about your business or staff?
4. In a perfect world, how would your clients describe you?
5. If I could provide a referral to solve your biggest **Pain Point**, what service would that be?

You may start with one of these questions and find yourself exploring a completely different topic or direction as you dive a little deeper into what your prospect needs. It is possible that your product or service isn't the best fit for them. Nevertheless, the time and energy that you spend developing relationships will keep the door open to referrals between the two of you.

Throw Away Questions

One of the quickest ways to lose a prospect is the overuse of **Throw Away Questions** in your conversations. It is OK to use them when they are relevant, but as your standard form of communication, they lack creativity, and originality.

- "Where are you from?"
- "What do you do?"
- "How long have you been in business?"

Your questions should be engaging, interesting, and always respectful of other people's time.

Respect People's Time

When YOU scheduled a meeting with someone and ask,

"How can we help you?"

That is a waste of another person's time. When you ask for an appointment, it is assumed that you have some ideas and solutions ready to deliver during the conversation. It is up to you to provide **value** when you request an audience with another person.

If you scheduled the meeting to find out ways you could support them, the following opening would be more appropriate:

"Thank you for seeing (or speaking with) me today. I know my company has some products and services that have served your industry well, but I would love to know a little more about your business, so I can see how we can provide even more support. May I ask you a few questions to get some additional clarity?"

Depending on your business, the line of questions might be completely different, but you can see the direction the conversation is taking. We are trying to provide **value** by understanding their true needs. Try using or adjusting some of the questions from the **Deeper Dive** section as a guideline.

Here is a quick reference list to help you utilize the **SKILL** of asking questions in your conversations.

1. Ask GREAT questions.
2. Provide VALUE.
3. Beware **TMI Syndrome.**
4. BUILD Relationships.
5. RESPECT other people's time.
6. LISTEN more than you talk.
7. Be AUTHENTIC.

Now that you've learned the basics of asking GREAT questions, you are going to put them to good use in the next chapter on **Rock Star Recruiting.**

Chapter 14

ROCK STAR RECRUITING

"Ask yourself if what you're doing today is getting
you closer to where you want to be tomorrow."
– Unknown

I n **Chapter 6: #RockThatDream Ridge**, I shared what inspired me to grow my team. Although the first recruit was slightly accidental, after that, they were all intentional. Meaning, I was motivated to help people enjoy more financial, personal, and developmental freedom. I wanted them to come with me, not only to **Success Island**, but all the way up **#RockThatDream Ridge**, to the **Pinnacle of Peace**. The view from the top is better when shared with others.

I realized early on that I needed to ASK EVERYONE. Not because I thought everyone was looking for a business, but because it was the polite thing to do. Yes, it is true, it is just plain old good manners.

If you have been holding yourself back from asking because you were worried about being rude or having others reject your hospitality, I want to share this with you...

Scene from a Dinner Party

You have invited a wonderful group of people over for a fabulous dinner party. Everyone is laughing, smiling, and having an excellent time. They enjoyed the food, the conversation, and the energy in the room. This is what connection is all about!

Then, it is time for dessert. The desserts look amazing, they smell delicious, and everyone is anxiously waiting for you to serve them up! You pick up your tray and start walking around the room eager to let your guests enjoy the delectable delights.

You stop in front of each person as they stare at the treats on your tray. Sharing your favorites and helping everyone decide which sweet treat they are ready to eat.

Eddie, Linda, and Molly each pick their favorites, ready to enjoy what you are offering. John and Jillian politely decline while April is excited to try one. You see Judy out of the corner of your eye and skip right past her without offering her anything.

Micki and Jason were full of objections about diets and how they "shouldn't", but after seeing the delight of others in the group, quickly changed their minds. Shelly and Oscar didn't need convincing, they were ready with forks in hand to dive-in and immediately start complimenting your offering.

You see the twins Millie and Mellie and you turn abruptly in the opposite direction and make a beeline towards Ronnie, who declines your offer. On the other hand, Amanda readily accepts with a grin and a giggle. You head back to the kitchen and as you pass back by John and Jillian, you ask once more, and Jillian changes her mind. She wants in on the excitement.

You brush past Nellie, Natasha, and Nathan and set the rest of the treats down out of their immediate reach on a table in the corner. There are forty guests here, but you have decided to offer your treats to only twelve. The rest of your guests feel insulted and ashamed that they weren't considered good enough to get a choice.

Can you imagine walking around the room eyeing each person individually and identifying who IS and who IS NOT worthy of receiving a dessert? Would you prejudge, predetermine, and preclude certain people as recipients for your treats?

Of course, not!

You probably understood the symbolism from that fictitious scene, that the dessert was your recruiting opportunity. You offered it to many. Some accepted, some declined, some objected, and some changed their minds. But, everyone who received the offer was thrilled because they got to make the choice. Those who were not offered anything felt disappointed and dejected- unworthy of the opportunity.

Obviously, you would never actually do that to your guests because it would be rude and offensive. So why would you withhold your recruiting opportunity?

When you are selling, we discussed in **Chapter 12: How to Be a Stellar Seller** that it is your JOB to present all the options to the buyer and to let them make an informed decision. It is also your JOB to share the career opportunity with others and let them decide if it is a good fit for them.

I can hear some of you now…

- I barely know what I am doing, I can't help someone else.
- I don't really understand the career opportunity, so I am afraid to try to share it effectively.
- People are too busy.
- The market is saturated.
- I'm not making any money yet, so I can't help them do it.

Those are what we call *your* objections and they are usually based in the **FEAR** we talked about in **Chapter 6: #RockThatDream Ridge**. I am going to help you overcome some of your objections in the next chapter, but for now, let's get back to the dessert analogy.

When we don't offer our opportunity to everyone, we are prejudging who will or won't be interested. When we offer the opportunity, people get to make their own choices. Recruiting, just like sales, is simply providing enough information for people to make an informed decision.

Remember my story about Cheryl? **"I was wondering if you were ever going to ask me. I didn't think you thought I could do it."**

You don't want to be guilty of making someone feel like you don't **Believe** in them or discouraging them from pursing their entrepreneurial **Dream**. So, do yourself a simple favor and ASK EVERYONE! The worst that can happen is they say "No", which is just a word. It has no personal reflection on you. The best that can happen is they say "Yes", and you can help them change their lives. I hope by the end of this chapter you will recognize it is worth the risk.

4 Magic Words

As a reminder, your first question starts with those 4 Magic Words: **Just out of curiosity...**

If you are shy, new to recruiting, or have difficulty with any lulls in conversation, your initial conversation might go, or might have gone, something like this...

> **You:** "**Just out of curiosity**, have you ever thought about doing something like this?"
>
> (One second of silence passes and you blurt out...)
>
> **You:** "If you haven't, I totally understand. I just wanted to mention it just in case. Give me a call if you change your mind."
>
> (You yell over your shoulder as you are running towards your car...)

I bet some of you laughed when you read that and thought, "Oh my goodness, I have totally done that!"

That is a classic example of what I call **Backpeddling**. It happens all the time. Any silence, including a micro pause, is interpreted as non-interest. That simply is not the case. It is **FEAR** that causes you to withdraw your offer before you get an answer. (Remember **FEAR of Rejection Road** in Chapter 6?)

Don't worry, I have a way to help you with your **Backpeddling**. It doesn't take any special tools or training. You have everything you need, with you right now. All you need to do is practice. Ready?

BYT

BYT stands for **B**ite **Y**our **T**ongue.

What? Bite my tongue?

Yes, I want you to **Bite Your Tongue**— not hard enough that it actually hurts. Just enough to remind you that there is a reason you are **not** going to fill the silence.

"Did you know that when you ask a question, the brain has an autonomic response that starts to formulate an answer?"

Let that sink in for a moment. Above, I asked you a question. If you read it with the correct punctuation, your brain would be making a split-second determination on whether you are familiar with that fact or not.

It isn't something that you can stop. It is **autonomic**, which means it is involuntary or being done unconsciously. Just like breathing, it happens without you thinking about it.

My point is, when you ask someone a question…

"Just out of curiosity, have you ever thought about doing something like this?"

Their brain autonomically starts to formulate an answer. The only thing that will stop this thought process is when it is interrupted. That is why you must **SHUT UP!** I know that sounds a little harsh, but it is true. You **MUST be quiet** and let the other person's brain formulate an answer to your question.

Statistically, the majority of the population in Northern America has thought about owning their own business at some point. If they weren't actively thinking about the opportunity before you asked the question, their brain will need to absorb that information before it can deliver an answer to you.

If they were actively thinking about it before you asked, the **Bully** is now telling them what a ridiculous idea it is. So, their brain is choosing whether it will be vulnerable and share the truth or let the **Bully** win.

When you interrupt their thoughts by asking another question, or just making small talk, you halt the process all together. It also takes you back to ground zero, to that moment before you got up the **Courage** to ask the question in the first place.

I understand it might get a little bit uncomfortable. Honestly, if you aren't used to it, silence is awkward and can be difficult to experience. However, I promise you, if you practice **BYT** to remind you to be quiet while they **think** about your question, they **will** answer you. Some of them will even say "Yes!"

Do you see how you can find out the person's interest level by keeping quiet? I have a lot more to teach you about recruiting in *DS 201* but for now, let's work on **Overcoming Objections**, which is the next step along your journey to **Success Island**.

Chapter 15

OVERCOMING OBJECTIONS

"An Objection is not a rejection;
it is simply a request for more information."
– Bo Bennett

O
vercoming **Objections** is a delicate process that usually involves working through multiple layers of confusion. As you resolve each concern, it is like peeling the layers that are preventing your prospect from making a choice. Eventually, you reach the core concern or true objection. Once it is exposed, it is typically easy to fix. That process is called **Peeling the Onion**. This chapter is designed to show you how to easily and skillfully identify the things that are holding people back from executing their decisions.

Now that you know how to ask a question and wait for an answer, it is time to resolve their concerns and potentially lead them to **Success Island**. Although we are talking about recruiting in this section, the methods I am going to share with you can be used for any conversation. These techniques will help you gain clarity and weed out the roadblocks that are coming between you and the joy of building your business. First, we need to start by handling what's holding **you** back.

YOUR Objections

It is important to address the concerns I mentioned in the last chapter. These are the things that could keep you from becoming a leader and exponentially increasing your income.

1. I barely know what I am doing, I can't help someone else.
2. I don't really understand the career opportunity. I am afraid to try to share it effectively.
3. People are too busy.
4. The market is saturated.
5. I'm not making any money yet, I can't help anyone else do it.

Objection #1—I barely know what I am doing, I can't help someone else.

I recognize that starting a business, especially in a new industry, can be a bit intimidating. You fell in love with the product, but wonder if you could really support somebody else when you feel like such a novice yourself.

Well, I have a solution for that called **Training in Tandem**. Your **Upline** leader can train you and your team member(s) at the same time. For example, when your **Downline** asks a question that you don't know the answer to, there is a simple response,

"Let me get back to you on that."

Your team members are not expecting you to have all the answers; they are expecting you to be a resource and to help them locate the information they need. When you find the answer, whether from your **Upline** leader or another source, you then relay the information to your team member(s). You will be learning right beside them, but still stabilizing your leadership skills by being the one that delivers the information. You are establishing your credibility and increasing your knowledge at the same time.

Objection #2—I don't really understand the career opportunity, so I am afraid to try to share it effectively.

The career opportunity can be a tricky thing even if you come from within the **DS** industry. There are terms and strategies that could be confusing for anyone. Earning personal promotions, tracking team members' requirements to stay active, or calculating bonuses can be difficult without a seasoned pro by your side. Your eyes may glaze over as you try to decipher the compensation plan, or as you ponder how many tiers or legs you need in order to be successful.

While you are learning the hierarchy of your company, make sure you have access to a leader who holds business opportunity meetings, so you can let them handle the heavy lifting while you are learning. Understand that means you participate in every call, meeting, and training available. You need to learn the comp plan and find an **Expert** to provide you with simple verbiage to teach your team. Duplication is your best friend in this industry

Objection #3—People are too busy.

People are busy; that is a fact. But, are you really the one to say if they are too busy, or should they be able to make that determination themselves? (Remember the **Scene from a Dinner Party**) This is often an excuse to cover up their true concern, which we will discuss more in the next section as we **Peel the Onion**.

We need to be honest and realize that we make time for things that are important to us. If your potential recruits are interested in doing this business and you need assistance showing them how to blend and prioritize their **Schedules**, there is a complete outline for you to teach them in the **NCT** Section in *DS 201*.

Objection #4—The market is saturated.

Here is the first thing I want you to remember.

"The market is only ever saturated, with mediocrity."

The **Sea of Mediocrity** is filled with average people with below average results. There are very few people who stand out in their efforts to build a business and a brand. I managed to recruit four people on the street I lived on within a six-house radius. We all had a circle of influence that overlapped, but we had a far greater one that was different.

If you continue reading this series of books, you will be able separate yourself from the pack and see a market that is NOT saturated. You will be consistently selling, scheduling, recruiting, and helping your own team members recognize the value of the **Market Separator**.

Objection #5—I'm not making any money yet, so I can't help them do it.

This can also be referred to as **Imposter Syndrome,** which I will discuss in more detail in **DS 201**. Ask yourself, "Has ANYONE ever made money in your company?" If they have, the resources are available to make it to **#RockThatDream Ridge** and when you are **Training in Tandem,** your team can join you on the journey.

If your company is new and no one has made money yet, you get to be the trailblazer in your industry. It is time for you to set your sails and lead others to **Stability Shore**. Until then, you can capitalize on the opportunity to be on the ground floor.

If you have more questions, Tweet me on Twitter **@VickiFitch** and use **#AskVicki**. I answer questions each week on my live broadcasts.

The Direct Sales industry is ripe with opportunities and training on products and services that can easily generate six-figure incomes and beyond.

"To make your Dreams come true, you must break free from the Sea of Mediocrity."

Breaking it Down

Remembering that this is still **Direct Selling 101,** I have broken the conversation down in simple layers in the following section. (I have saved the detailed conversations for **DS 201**) Now that we have addressed **your** Objections, it's time to start focusing on the ones you will hear from others.

At the end of **Chapter 15: Rock Star Recruiting**, I posed a question. Now I'm providing you with the correct reply…

> **"Just out of curiosity**, have you ever thought about doing something like this?"
>
> **Yes**—"Great! What is holding you back?"
>
> (This is where their list of objections comes in.)
>
> **No**—"Really? Why?"
>
> (This is where their list of objections comes in.)

Both answers make it easy for you to segue into **Overcoming Objections**.

The next five words I teach you will change your life. I know that sounds kind of dramatic, but it is still true. If you use them and practice the **BYT** Method, you will change the sales & recruiting success in your business. Are you ready?

"If I could… would you?"

It is such a simple question, but WOW are these words powerful. When we use this question to **Peel the Onion**, we will discover the true objections of the client, without the conversation turning into what some might consider, an "argument".

Here is an example of a conversation with great intentions…

> **You:** "**Just out of curiosity**, have you ever thought about doing something like this?"
>
> **Them**: "My husband would never be supportive."
>
> **You:** "Of course he would, especially when you show him how much money you can make."
>
> **Them**: "Actually, I am too busy."
>
> **You:** "I have a team member who has seven children, and she finds time to work it in. I know you can, too!"

Them: "I don't even have any money to get started."

You: "This business is going to make you money. You can't afford NOT to get started."

Some of those objections and answers might sound familiar to you. You may have used them on someone else, or someone may have used them on you. Either way, they are not the most effective way of helping others see the potential of joining your team.

First, you aren't really hearing the person you are talking to. It is important that people feel heard and understood, but your replies are discarding their concerns with answers that satisfy **you**. The lack of validation would be discouraging, and conversations that go back and forth like that can be exhausting.

By the third objection, they will start to get tired of this discussion. It is possible that some people will cave-in and sign up just to get you to stop badgering them. I assume that is not the type of team member you are looking for. The other alternative is they start avoiding you because you made them feel uncomfortable. You may even develop a reputation for not caring about other people's feelings.

That doesn't mean it is true, but it is harder to undo a bad reputation than it is to do it right in the first place. If you already have a reputation for this type of behavior, never fear; we will help you respectfully **Overcome the Objections** and deliver the new and improved version of yourself to your prospects. That being said, let's get back to those five little words, so I can help you *#RockThatDream*.

Peeling the Onion

The art of using the *"If I could... would you?"* method is an effective way to **Peel the Onion**. It will help you to clearly see the true objection that might be holding your potential recruit from joining you.

When we listen to people and understand their concerns, we have a chance to fill in the **FEAR** with truth, so we know if what we have to offer is a good fit.

In my experience, it usually takes about three layers of the onion before I actually encounter the true objection that is preventing them from moving forward. It is important to validate the concern, and then **Peel the Onion** by asking a question.

Here is the conversation from the previous section, modified using the *"If I Could... Would You?"* Method...

NOTE: You will notice **Layer 2** uses the exact phraseology *If I Could... Would You?* The other layers have been slightly modified for more meaningful conversation, but you can see the premise is the same. Changing the *"I could"* for *"you had"*, etc.

"Just out of curiosity, have you ever thought about doing something like this?"

Layer 1:

Them: "My husband would never be supportive."

You: "I understand where that would be important to you. So, *if you had* your husband's support, then *would you* be interested?"

Layer 2:

Them: "Actually, I am too busy."

You: "I understand. Having a balanced schedule is really important to me too. So, *if I could* show you how to work this into your current schedule without you feeling stressed out, *would you* be interested?"

Layer 3:

Them: "I don't even have any money to get started."

You: "I completely understand and want to help you build that financial freedom. So, *if I could* show you how to get the money without dipping into your family budget, then *would you* be interested?"

Resolution:

Them: "Yes, I would."

You: "Great, let's talk about a few solutions and find one that works for you."

The third or fourth question is usually when they will reveal the true concern or objection. Keep in mind, it may take more than three layers. However, you don't need to answer any questions until you get an actual response.

As a quick reminder, *DS 201* includes the details on how to answer the objection brought up in the Resolution stage of the conversation, as well as transition phrasing to get your paperwork signed or the online application filled out. That being said, I have something URGENT to bring to your attention. Many "authorities" preach the opposite of what I am about to say. Their error could be holding you back from reaching **Success Island**.

EXPECT the YES!

Some of the most exasperating things I hear from other professionals or leaders are…

"Expect the No."

"Aim for 100 No's."

In my opinion, that is poor advice. You know what happens when you "Expect the No"?

You get it!

Yes, that is right. When you expect the "No", more often than not, you get it.

And when you get the unexpected "Yes", you know what comes out of your mouth? One single word that makes people rethink their previous declaration. Without meaning to, you question their decision by blurting out… "**Really?**"

Not because you don't think it is a good opportunity, but because your defense mechanism was prepared and ready for the "No" so you are slightly (or greatly) surprised because your **Expectation** is to always be turned down. This practice may result in you talking yourself out of the sale, the recruit, or the traffic ticket. (Just kidding—I wanted to make sure you were still paying attention.)

Yes, this happens all the time. Trust me, I've seen it live and in person. I've coached it over and over again. Your new motto should be:

"Expect the Yes!"

Not to be confused with the **Expectation** that the client is going to purchase. It means to be prepared for the positive outcome.

You have a great product and a great opportunity, so start acting like it!

When we **Expect the Yes**, we will start to receive it more often, and we need to be prepared to execute the request and move forward immediately. **Experts** are always prepared with the paperwork, the link, or the products that were requested, whenever possible. When you **Expect the Yes** and are prepared, you are displaying **Confidence,** which will make it easier for others to follow your lead.

There will also be times when the prospect is interested but isn't ready to move forward immediately. That brings us to our next chapter, understanding how fortunes are lost or made.

Chapter 16

THE FORTUNE IS IN THE FOLLOW UP

"The riches are in the niches,
but the Fortune is in the Follow Up.
– Pat Flynn

One of the best kept secrets of **Success Island** is the **Follow Up Ferry**. It runs every day like clockwork. It is accessible to everyone and is never crowded, yet few people ever use it. This chapter is dedicated to helping you utilize this resource because... The Fortune is in the **Follow Up**.

Hearing this phrase and understanding it are two completely different things. As you know from **Chapter 2: My Story**, I started my first company with employees when I was twenty years old. What you don't know is how that business started, and what I had to do to get it off the ground.

Back in the day, yes, I am dating myself, there was no **Social Media**, and the internet didn't exist yet. I had quit my well-paying job to start my own company just six months after purchasing my first home. Needless to say, money was tight, and I had no advertising budget. I built my entire business on cold calls from the **FBN** (Fictitious Business Name) Statement listings.

This was a bit like déjà vu, since that is exactly how I started when I was twelve, by getting people to accept free insurance quotes. The difference this time was that there was something significant riding on it. It wasn't a phone line in a teenager's room; it was a house payment, and the bank would definitely notice if I missed that!

Those **FBN** listings were like little nuggets of gold. Daily phone calls with effective and efficient **Follow Up** were all I had to generate revenue for my business. I won't go into all the details, but if you read the second chapter, you know it turned out pretty well for me.

The **Follow Up** process is an important part of sales. Check out these statistics!

Follow Up Statistics	
78%	Don't Follow Up
20%	Make 1-3 Calls
1.5%	Make 4-6 Calls
<.5%	Make 7 + Calls
To make a SALE you must	**Make 7-15 Calls**

So, what does that mean to you? That means that even if you didn't have any additional training and you weren't even particularly good at your job, you could push yourself to the top .5% of the world as long as you are persistent!

That should encourage you by reminding you that you CAN do it. **Persistence** wins out! Does that mean you should kickback and settle yourself in for the 7-15 call **Follow Up** journey? Of course not. If you implement the things I am teaching in this book series, you will significantly cut that down and will often find yourself with a **First Call Close**. But the times that you do have to **Follow Up**, you need to remember this:

Follow Up Until...

Until what? I don't remember where I originally heard this, and I offer my apologies to the original author. The next phrase is completely **Tongue in Cheek**, so please don't send me any hate mail. Just know that it is meant to be humorous and to express a point.

"Follow Up until... they Buy, Die, or Tell you to go away."

Let's look at what that phrase is really saying. It isn't saying stalk people. (I have a great article on **Follow Up**, including the schedule I use at **www.VickiFitch. com/DS101**.) It is suggesting that when someone expresses an interest in our products, we should **Follow Up** until they **tell** us they are no longer interested. We know people are busy, and **Experts** know that people appreciate **Follow Up** because it is a form of customer service.

Why then is it so hard for us to pick up the phone? (Yes, the phone. I recognize that in this day and age of technology and texting, some people think we should get away from that. But I can prove to you in *DS 201* that the **Phone is Your Friend**.) The simple answer? Going back to that 4-Letter "F" Word, **FEAR**.

1. **FEAR** of Rejection.
2. **FEAR** of Judgment.
3. **FEAR** of bothering them or them thinking you are "pushy".
4. **FEAR** of not remembering what you promised or why you are calling.
5. **FEAR** of not remembering who they are or where you met them.

It all starts out by addressing our **FEAR** of **Follow Up**, so let's review a scenario that might give you some perspective.

If you have a friend whose child has a serious case of eczema, and you knew of a product to help, would you tell them or keep it a secret? The obvious answer is you would tell them.

Would you hesitate to call and find out if the product worked? I wouldn't think so. Checking in is part of friendship. There is no **Expectation** of the outcome; it is simply because you care.

Our **FEAR** comes when there is potential benefit for us. Worrying about what they will think.

- What if they don't like it?
- What if they think I don't care but am just trying to sell them something?
- What if they don't want to talk to me anymore?

Understanding the **FEAR** and **Reframing** it is the best way to change your perspective.

An **Expectation** is something you strongly **Believe** will happen.

When you SHARE with your friends, you have no **Expectation**.

Without the **Expectation**, there is no letdown, embarrassment, or rejection.

Without the possibility of letdown, embarrassment or rejection, there is no **FEAR**.

So, one might deduce that without **Expectation** there is no **FEAR**.

"When you are sharing to SERVE
instead of SELL,
you remove the FEAR."

When your perspective changes, you recognize **Follow Up** is a way to SERVE others and is actually a sign that you care.

Have you ever wanted or needed something, but kept putting it off because your schedule was so busy you never made time to finish the process or make the purchase? I have done so on a number of occasions. I was thrilled that the person continued to **Follow Up** with me until I was able to complete the transaction or get my questions answered.

Facing FEAR

To emphasize this point and how it actually benefits others, let's review this scenario again.

You are involved with a company that has an amazing product for eczema. You have seen results, heard the testimonials, and have complete confidence in its ability to help.

You hear about the difficulty your friend's child is having with eczema (**Pain Point**) and you provide her a sample of the product (**Solution**) to see if it works for her. What do you do next?

If you are most people, you probably fall into one of these scenarios…

- You hope that she will call you to rave about the product and place an order.
- You send a text or email, requesting a phone call, if she has any questions.
- You tell her that she can buy it at cost because you aren't in this business for the money.
- You never **Follow Up**, assuming it didn't work, or she isn't interested.

If you can relate to any of those examples, don't feel guilty or ashamed. Just recognize there is a better way. One of the easiest ways to feel confident on a **Follow Up** call is to schedule a next action date while you are talking to the person.

For example, when you provide the sample of your product, select a date and time the following week to **Follow Up** and find out if they liked it and/or to get their opinion. When you schedule an appointment, they will be expecting your call.

"ALWAYS set a next action date to keep
FEAR out of your Follow Up."

---

*NOTE: If you forgot to schedule a next action date, or you have a stack of old calls to make, I go into more details in **DS 201** of how to handle those. For now, remember that by investing your time in reaching out, you are serving them and honoring their busy **Schedules**.*

I understand that when you pick up the phone to **Follow Up**, the **Bully in Your Head** might start to whisper (or yell) things like,

- You are bothering them.
- They aren't interested, or they would have called you.
- When they say they are busy or ask you to call back, that's code for "I don't want what you have."
- They didn't like the product and don't want to tell you.
- They don't like you as a person.

You will learn more how to handle that **Bully** in *Evict the Bully in Your Head*. For now, just trust me and remember that following up is a sign of caring and providing great Customer Service.

Speaking of Customer Service, have I got a story for you....

Chapter 17

CRUSHING IT IN CUSTOMER SERVICE

"Building a good customer experience doesn't
happen by accident. It happens by design."
— **Clare Muscutt**

Now that you understand the power of the **Follow Up Ferry**, I want to introduce you to a very popular destination on **Success Island.** Nestled off the edge of the **Sea of Tranquility** is the **Entrepreneurial Theme Park**. Inside the Park, you will find a fun-loving place called the **Customer Service Carnival**. While you are here, the staff looks for ways to make you happy, help you win prizes, and make sure you go home with everything you want. The goal at the Carnival is for you to share your experience with all your friends and leave with the esteemed **Raving Fan** pin, which identifies you as a very happy Customer.

I recommend that all new Entrepreneurs spend time here at the **Customer Service Carnival** to learn to right way to treat your Customers. The story I am about to share with you exemplifies what happens if you skip the Carnival. It isn't a pretty picture.

As you know from an earlier chapter, the trip I took to finalize this book ended up being my starting point. It could have derailed me from my mission, goal, and objective, but it didn't. However, the experience I had at the hotel almost did.

Hotel Hell

Writing a book is quite a project. Personally, due to my desire to write quickly, I typically go away for four or five days to write and complete my projects. I have a few specifications to be as productive as possible.

- Quiet Location
- Good Wi-Fi
- Desk with Comfortable Chair
- Refrigerator, Microwave, and Coffee Pot
- Gym with a Treadmill and Hot Tub
- Early Check in and Late Check Out

My husband usually handles my travel arrangements and verifies the details before selecting a hotel. I was squeezing this trip in between two others with moving timelines, so he did the recon and I just needed to finalize it once the other itineraries were confirmed.

The following is the mostly unedited account of what happened to me while I was there. Now that you are properly prepped and know where the story starts… enjoy!

Day Before Arrival

Once my other itineraries were confirmed, I called the hotel to provide the credit card information to make my reservation official. Vicki answered the phone (easy to remember that name), and said, "Oh, you can secure it now, but there is no need, we have plenty of room. You can just come in tomorrow."

OK, you probably know that my first thought was, "I need to go do sales training at this hotel." You ALWAYS want to secure your reservations with payment. Having a person's information in the computer isn't the same as having a credit card guaranteeing the stay. It is also a great chance to gather additional information, so you can provide exemplary customer service.

I confirmed all the details my husband had discussed on the phone, including the amenities, arrival and departure dates, rates, etc. Vicki confirmed them and assured me it was all in the computer. I could just check in the following day, no problem.

On her recommendation, I decided not to provide the credit card. My intention was to use it as an example when I suggested my sales training to the manager. (Yes, you should always think about how you can provide your products and services to people who need them). This was where things got interesting...

Day One

I showed up at 2pm on Thursday and got the unique privilege of meeting Lydia. Lydia was a lovely Asian woman with a thick accent that made check-in a bit less smooth than I would have enjoyed. I explained I had spoken to Vicki the day before and that my tentative reservation was in the computer. I told her I was checking in until Monday to finish my book and she was excited to tell me that it was her **Dream** to write a book. I recommended she pursue that and start writing, which made her smile.

She proceeded to tell me about the rate increase for Friday & Saturday nights, due to it being a weekend, and gave me the total of my bill. I nodded, handing her my credit card. Then, things got confusing.

She handed me a card about their frequent visitor's program, (great customer service and sales suggestion here) and told me I could get a Free Upgrade by joining. This was our conversation:

Me: "Great!" I said as I pulled out my phone to do it.

Lydia: "No! Not right now."

Me: "Oh, I thought you said I could get a free upgrade."

Lydia: "Sometimes you can."

Me: "Is now one of those times?"

Lydia: "I don't know."

Me: "Oh, well how do we find out?"

Lydia: "I don't know."

Me: "Oh, so should I try and see if it works?"

Lydia: "I don't know, I don't think so."

Me: "Hmmm, I'm getting confused. If I sign up for your program, will I get a free upgrade?"

Lydia: "Yes, sometimes."

Me: "Could now be one of those times?"

Lydia: "I don't know."

Me: "OK, well I'm getting rather confused. Let's just forget it for now, so I can get up to my room and get to work."

Lydia: "Oh, well if you want a room upstairs, it is going to cost more."

Me: "What?"

Lydia: "I have a room for your right here on the 1st floor."

Me: "OK, then I want to get OVER to my room. Is it quiet there?"

Lydia: "Yes, that is the quiet side."

(Now, I was nervous that there was a non-quiet side, but OK. I smiled and nodded.)

She had me sign the paper that said I would not smoke or bring any pets in.

No Smoking… Check.

No Pets… Check.

Here alone, no pets, and no smoking. We were good to go. I took my two keys and found out there was no bellman, so I headed outside to get my luggage.

NOTE TO SELF: Add Bellman to your list of requirements.

I got my first load of luggage… OK don't judge. The cart was small, and I drink A LOT of water. I also needed snacks, my computer, other electronic devices, etc… again no judging. I am a Girl Scout by nature.

I came back in the door with the wobbly luggage cart and headed down the hall to my room. When I arrived and slid my key into the slot, I was disappointed to find that my key would not work. I tried it several more times, to no avail. Hoping it was just a faulty magnetic strip on that card, I pulled out the other one and tried again. No dice, it was not working.

My rocking cart and I wandered back up the hall to the front desk, and one of my baskets landed on the floor with a thud as some of my things went elegantly rolling down the hallway. I scrambled to pick them up before everyone in the lobby saw me chasing my water bottles.

I approached the front counter again and let Lydia know the key was not working. She apologized profusely and handed me a new set of keys right away.

Feeling a little concerned about the stability of my cart, I repositioned a few things and headed back down the corridor again. To my dismay, there was still, as they say in the military, no joy.

Seriously?

Was there something wrong with me that I could not slide this electronic key properly into the assigned slot? I travel extensively, so I felt fairly competent in the art of opening an electronic door but perhaps there was something different here.

I tried repeatedly, looking for the lights. In case you aren't familiar, a red light means the key doesn't work (or you are trying to enter the wrong room… don't ask me how I know that!) The green light means you are cleared for entrance. Upon further inspection of this door, there was no light. Several more tries and I chalked it up to a faulty card reader.

I headed back up the hallway. Starting to feel the frustration of the missing computer file and the tumbling basket combined with the circumstances of my numerous trips up and down this hallway, I began to feel my energy fade...

"**Make your Move,** Vicki!" I said to myself. I didn't want this to throw off my day. **#Brightside** I was getting in extra steps for the day.

With a slightly better state of mind, I hurried back up the hallway to connect with my new bestie, Lydia.

> **Me:** "The key still doesn't work." I told her with the best smile I could produce.
>
> **Lydia:** "Oh no, let me make some more keys and I'll come with you this time."
>
> **Me:** "OK." I was keeping Tony Robbins in mind, remembering it is important to "Change your state."

So, for the fifth time down this familiar corridor, we arrived at the room.

Lydia, with full confidence, and possibly a little bit of expectation that I was inept at opening doors, slid the key in and bumped the door with her shoulder as she turned the handle.

THUD went Lydia's shoulder against the door. It didn't budge.

> **Lydia:** "I am so sorry. Let's go fix this."

"Yes, let's do that," I thought to myself as I balanced that unsteady basket again on top of my suitcase, hoping it doesn't tumble off again. My thoughts wandered to how helpful a bellman would have been at this point, as I made my sixth trip back up this corridor. Truthfully, my joy was waning, but I plastered a semi-fake smile on my face. (I'm being honest here!)

When we arrived back at the familiar landing place of the front desk, Lydia surprised me...

> **Lydia:** "I'm going to give you a free upgrade!" She announced this with a beaming smile on her face.

Me: "Thank you." I said as I thought to myself, that seems like the right thing to do anyway based on our earlier conversation.

She proceeded to pull out her paperwork and assign me to a new room. (I didn't realize at the time that this new upgrade was NOT on the quiet side of the hotel—we will talk about that later.)

She crossed out the original room number on the paper I had signed and handed me the keys. I looked at her a little puzzled because I somewhat expected her to come with me to make sure they worked.

Me: "Are you sure these are going to work?"

Lydia: "Of course!"

I nodded and smiled. (I had a feeling if I could have seen my own face, it would have looked a tad skeptical. Nonetheless, I proceeded to push my wiggly cart to the elevator doors and head on up to the fourth floor.)

Getting to the door, I slid my key in and bumped my own shoulder against it as I turned the handle.

It didn't work…

I literally looked around the hallway for some hidden cameramen, expecting them to pop out at any moment saying I am getting "Punked". This MUST be a joke…

Recognizing that some doors are temperamental, I kept putting the key in the door and sliding it over and over. I realized that no lights were coming on here either. Saying a quick prayer, I kept wiggling and putting it in and pulling it out at varying degrees. Just as I was about to walk away and scream, I tried one more time with a quick flip and swish motion, and it miraculously opened… (Thank you Jesus!)

I quickly entered the room, lost in thought, wondering if I was going to be battling with the lock every time I left. I was quickly brought back to reality as my entrance was met with some of the loudest traffic I have ever heard in my life.

Upon a quick inspection, I noticed the windows had been left wide open. Deep inside, I was secretly hoping that the sound would completely fade away when they were closed. Unfortunately, that was not the case. Closing the windows slightly muffled the whizzing traffic but in no way provided serenity in the room. Touting close freeway proximity was only a bonus for driving, not for resting. I was so close to the freeway, I think I could have picked out my neighbor driving by.

I will not lie, by this time I was very frustrated. Since I am a proponent of **#BrightSide** thinking, I reminded myself I was on a mission and I needed to get busy. I closed the window, unpacked my things, and took a quick walk to find the gym and spa before I got settled in.

I headed downstairs in the elevator and discovered that the gym and pool were just a short distance away from the wayward room I was now longing for on the "quiet side" of the hotel. It was like walking by someone that had rejected you and wishing for a moment that you could reconnect, so you could make things alright again.

I passed my nemesis room and found the gym, or what they were calling a gym. There was a treadmill in there but for some reason, they had removed the TV and left a large cable swinging from the wall. The indoor pool and spa were right next door, separated only by a clear glass wall. I headed out to the spa to feel the temperature as I thought about lowering my body into the hot water and letting the jets beat the tension that had built up out of my shoulders.

As I opened the door, I heard that same annoying whizzing sound that was coming from the open window in my room! This "indoor" pool, as they were calling it, included a room and three and a half walls. There was a completely exposed wrought iron style gate separating this pool from the outside world. The freeway traffic came barreling in and bouncing off the walls like a never-ending echo chamber.

I walked over to slip my hand in the water to check the temperature and found that it was not hot. It was more like a very warm bath. The next thing I saw left me feeling a bit uneasy. There was some unidentified debris at the bottom of the spa. I can only describe them as looking like a family of extra-large dust bunnies. I had absolutely no idea what they were made of, but I had to assume all of it had blown in from the open slats in the gate. I was thinking to myself, if I was a secret shopper reviewing this hotel, the only way to describe it would be "A Hot Mess of a hotel."

I know you are all wondering why I didn't run for the hills. It would seem like I am a glutton for punishment. But my real motivation was completing this book. Once I set my mind to doing something, I like to see it through. Plus, after evaluating the time to pack up, find another location, get there, and get settled in again, it seemed like I would waste the precious time I had.

As an entrepreneur, I always want to give people and places the benefit of the doubt and give them a chance to fix things that are going wrong. I've built and sold four successful companies, and I have had my share of employees that could have run off customers if a customer had not been kind enough to tell me how they were behaving. Of course, in the spirit of entrepreneurship, I went to the front desk and tried to discreetly share my findings with Lydia. I quietly had the following conversation:

> **Me:** "Lydia, I went to the indoor pool area, and the spa needs to be cleaned."
>
> **Lydia:** "You want me to switch your room again?"
>
> **Me:** "What? No. The spa is dirty." I said as I pointed down the hall to the Indoor Pool.
>
> **Lydia:** "What's wrong with your room?"
>
> **Me:** "There is nothing wrong with my room. There is something in the bottom of the Jacuzzi that needs to be cleaned, so I can go in it." I was cupping my hands in her direction so no one else could hear me.
>
> **Lydia:** "What room would you like?"
>
> **Me:** "What? I don't want another room…" My voice trailed off as I saw her bewildered look. "Never mind…" I walked off toward the elevator.

There is something to be said for making sure your staff truly understands the primary language spoken in the country. Now, don't get me wrong. I have no problem with people who are learning. I would want grace if I was in a different country where the primary language was different than my own. However, I probably wouldn't have them be the first line of customer service in my organization. Staying at a hotel is supposed to be easy. This was painful.

This hotel was only a year old and was actually a lovely place aesthetically. Just to be clear, it was not some run down "No Tell, Motel." The entrepreneur in me also was keenly aware that by staying, there was an opportunity here for me to consult with them and do some training. At the very least, it would make good conversation for my speaking engagements. I decided to just go back to my room and get busy.

Returning to the room gave me another dose of the loud and irritating freeway, but I got myself settled in and started writing. I worked hard, taking breaks to stretch, drink water, and get my blood pumping. I was in the groove. During one of my breaks at around 11pm, I decided to get ready for bed. While sorting through my toiletries bag, I realized I had forgotten my toothbrush. I called down to the front desk to see if I could get a toothbrush sent up...

> **Me:** "I am so sorry, I just realized I forgot my toothbrush, can you send one up to my room please?"
>
> **Front Desk:** "We don't provide toothbrushes, but you can purchase one for $2."
>
> **Me:** "Are you kidding? I am a guest at your hotel for five days and you can't provide me a toothbrush?"
>
> **Front Desk:** "I'm sorry, no, you will have to purchase it." The answer came in a matter of fact tone.
>
> **Me:** "I think this is ridiculous, but I am not going to argue. Fine, please charge it to my room and send it up."
>
> **Front Desk:** "No, you have to come down and get it."
>
> **Me:** "Really? I have to change out of my pajamas to come down and get it?" I said this with a mounting frustration that felt like Mt. St. Helens was ready to erupt.
>
> **Front Desk:** "I'm sorry, but yes." No empathy or concern, just facts.

Me: "Oooo Kaay…" I said in an obviously irritated voice. "I'll be right down."

Being a proponent of **#BrightSide** thinking, I started rattling off a list:

- Extra steps!
- Makes for a good chapter in a book!
- Great funny story or conversation starter!
- This will be funny another day!
- Opportunity to consult and train here on customer service, sales, marketing, and branding. This place is a GOLDMINE of problems!

I got dressed and headed down to the front desk for my toothbrush. I walked up to the counter with a fake smile plastered back on my face,

Me: "Hi, I'm Vicki Fitch. I called about the toothbrush."

Terrance: "$2 please." He says as he pulls the package from behind the counter and lays it on top close to himself. He was guarding this coveted resource like a lion protecting a cub.

Me: "Just charge it to my room please." I said as I reached for the toothbrush.

Terrance: "No." He answered with a straight face as he pulled it back towards himself.

Me: "What? Why?"

Terrance: "We don't do that."

Me: "I don't have $2. I don't have any cash with me. I changed out of my pajamas to get a toothbrush." I think the vein on my forehead was starting to throb.

Front Desk: "I'm sorry."

Me: "SERIOUSLY????" I am now ready to lose it.

Terrance: "Can't you go to an ATM?" He replies as if it is a normal request for a woman to leave a hotel at almost midnight in search of an ATM, so she can brush her teeth.

Me: "You want me to leave the hotel at 11:30pm at night to find an ATM to give you $2 for a toothbrush?"

Terrance: "Yes."

Me: "You have got to be kidding me!!!" I have admittedly raised my voice now. "I've never had to pay for a toothbrush before in a hotel, and now you want me to do what?"

Terrance, the representative at the front desk, was an Asian man likely in his forties. At some point in his customer service life, he should have been taught it is OK to make a $2 decision to assist a guest, especially one who is staying five days & four nights in your hotel. Apparently, that was not part of his training experience because he was quite perplexed and looked to a young man who was probably in his twenties and said…

Terrance: "What do we do?"

Me: "What you SHOULD do is provide a toothbrush to your customer, so they can brush their teeth, without having to consult another person in the hotel. Since that seems uncomfortable for you, is there a manager I can speak to?" I was no longer stunned by the lack of ability of the staff. I have accepted that the entire staff must be new because there is no other explanation of why the hotel is still in business.

Terrance: "Yes." He says to the younger man, "Go call the manager. He will know what to do."

I waited, and waited, and waited. Just as I was ready to use a facecloth as my toothbrush for the evening, the young man came out of the back and said,

2nd Person: "Just give her the toothbrush."

Terrance: "You'll go to the ATM tomorrow and bring the money back?"

With a look of astonishment on my face. I took my toothbrush without answering and went to my room.

No matter how positive you are, this kind of day can really get on your nerves. On my way back up the elevator, I started thinking about how many times I was going to be sharing this story in the future and that I had nicknamed this **Hotel Hell**. Little did I know, it was going to get worse.

When I got back to my room, I was greeted by the symphony of traffic still streaming by on the freeway. I continued working until about 1am where I was forced to use my earplugs and Pandora in order to get to sleep. I drifted off, praying that tomorrow would be better.

Day Two

The next morning, when I woke up, I hit it hard again. I drowned out the sounds of the traffic with a little background music and a lot of concentration. I was progressing steadily and decided I would go get something to eat and take a break when housekeeping came to clean the room. I continued working and they did not come. I kept on working, and they still did not come. I ate snacks and coffee in the morning but eventually, I decided to go out and get some food at around 2pm.

There was a restaurant on the same property, but not in the hotel. (Another question I should have asked about was food and room service, but I thought that was a given... My bad—Lesson learned). I walked to the restaurant and ate a delicious meal from a waitress named Bunnie, who was very helpful and cooperative.

Now refreshed after a good meal, I was charged up and ready to write! I walked back over to the hotel, where I discovered there was a back door that was closer to the restaurant. I slid my card into the lock three times but all I saw was a red light. Seriously, the hotel isn't that old... did they just put faulty equipment in everywhere?

Make your Move! Someday this would be funny and not infuriating!

As I started to walk all the way around the building to get to the front entrance, another gentleman staying in the hotel took out his key and opened the door for me.

I walked up to the front desk and guess who's back? My pal Lydia.

Me: "Hi Lydia, my key won't work again."

Lydia: "I know, that is because check out was at 12 noon."

Me: "Lydia, I am staying until Monday, remember? You checked me in." I was fully expecting her to apologize for the error.

Lydia: "Well, that isn't what this paper says." She sneered. ". The one you signed."

Me: "You mean the one you gave me to sign about the no pets and no smoking rules after you confirmed the nightly rate difference of weekday and weekend rates? The one you had me sign after you quoted me the rate for the entire stay, just to make sure I wasn't confused by the increase in rate on the weekend?" I asked just a tad sarcastically.

Lydia: "Well, you signed it."

Me: "Well, I guess we need to fix that since I am staying until Monday." I have now given up on any conversations with Lydia that should even slightly resemble logic.

Lydia: "You will have to move rooms then."

Me: "WHAT????" I exclaim, trying to keep my cool.

Lydia: "Otherwise, I am charging you $40 more per night for the upgrade."

Me: "WHAT????" I was now staring at her with a look that I'm sure wasn't very becoming. I thought about doing a **Livestream**… "Live from **Hotel Hell!**"

Lydia: "You didn't like the first room, so we moved you, but now you have to pay the upgrade if you want to stay in there."

Me: "ARE YOU KIDDING ME???? First of all, I NEVER SAW the first room because the door wouldn't open. Second of all, you KNEW how long I was staying and third of all, I AM NOT MOVING, and I am NOT paying you any additional money per night."

(Admittedly, I was no longer in my calmest state.)

Lydia: "There is no reason to raise your voice."

Me: "Let me speak to your manager, please."

Lydia: "How about I let you stay in your room for a while, and I will speak to my manager?"

Me: "That is a lovely idea." I said gritting my teeth. "Is this key going to work?"

Lydia: "No, let me give you a new one." I was experiencing déjà vu. At this point, I had accepted that this was par for the course at this hotel. No one even seemed slightly concerned at the constant stream of problems.

I was mildly seething as I went up the elevator. The key was requiring me to do another round of gymnastics to get it to work. I heard the phone ringing in the room and since I literally just left the lobby, it seems hard to believe that Lydia is already expecting me to have miraculously flown past the elevator to have gotten into the room that fast.

Lydia: "You can stay in that room for no extra charge per night. Rest for a while and then come down and give me your credit card." She stated bluntly without a hint of being sorry for all the trouble she had caused.

Me: "I will be back down later this evening when I go to eat dinner. I need to get back to writing." I clarified with her, still unsure why I had to give her my credit card again.

Lydia: "OK."

Thirty-five minutes later, the phone rang… It was Terrance.

Terrance: "When are you coming to bring your credit card?"

Me: "Later tonight, like I told Lydia. When I go to eat dinner, I will come down. I am really trying to focus on my book and would prefer not being disturbed."

Terrance: "OK, we will see you later."

Now in all honesty, my state of mind was currently tanked. I was frustrated, irritated, and thinking about moving hotels. Identifying all the reasons why somewhere else would make sense, I called my husband and shared the craziness of my time so far. Needless to say, he was in shock. He set out to find another hotel that was close by, so I didn't have to waste any more time. He found me a place we had stayed before that was a little farther away in the opposite direction. But, he was confident that it would meet my needs.

As one last move to give this place a chance to fix things before I shared my experience and what a nightmare this place was, I called the front desk and asked to speak to the manager. Terrance answered the phone.

Me: "Hi Terrance, this is Vicki Fitch. I would like to speak to the manager on duty please."

Terrance: "Oh, OK. He is on the phone right now, can I have him call you back?"

Me: "Of course, you know where I am." I replied, wondering if I would ever actually get a return call.

A short time later, the phone rang. It was Jason, the hotel manager.

I proceeded to share my incredulous story of being in this hotel, sparing some of the details but making sure the general exasperation was clear. I told him I was giving them one more chance to fix it before I left for another hotel.

Surprisingly, Jason apologized for what had happened, promised to train the staff better to handle these situations, and asked me to stay. As his exceptional way of handling the situation, he offered me a fifty percent discount off my room for the previous night.

I tried to be gracious. I didn't have the heart to tell him that was actually a bit of an insult considering what I had been through. In the customer service world, he should have offered me my entire stay for free, just so news of this experience would never hit the streets.

1. Faulty door locks
2. TVs missing from the walls
3. Dust bunny invasions in the spa
4. Incredible levels of noise in the rooms and the pool.
5. Getting locked out of the hotel because of the incompetence of the front desk staff
6. Toothbrush incident

None of these would go over well with the public as individual challenges, but adding them all together and announcing it would have proven catastrophic for a hotel in such a tight knit community.

Keeping the sarcasm from my voice, I made a suggestion.

> **Me:** "Jason, at the VERY LEAST you should offer me the entire night's stay free of charge considering the challenges I've been through."
>
> **Jason:** "I need to clear that with my manager."

"Oh my…" I thought to myself. "There is no one in this entire establishment, including managers, that can make customer service decisions without consulting with someone else. How do they function?"

He called back shortly to let me know he had cleared it with his manager, and again asked me to come down with my credit card. I agreed to be down when my family came to have dinner with me.

When I arrived downstairs, I approached the front desk and found Terrance was there to greet me and take my credit card info again. He was beaming with pride as he handed me a copy of the bill for the previous night's stay, which was supposed to have been zeroed out per Jason. He slid the document over for me to sign and as I looked down, I literally burst out laughing.

Although Terrance had cleared the balance for the hotel room, he had figured out how to charge me $2 for the toothbrush. I was honestly stunned at first. Then, I just recognized that this hotel could be an entire book on customer service and what NOT to do when trying to build a business.

I had no more strength or energy to address this anymore and was no longer going to spend any more time trying to understand the penny-wise and pound-foolish nature of the way they ran this hotel. Inside, I was wondering if Jason actually knew about this, or if Terrance just take it upon himself to learn something new. Either way, I really didn't want to take the look of joy off his face, so I just signed the credit card slip and went on my merry way.

This was my motto coming to life right in front of me. There is always *Profit in the Pain*. In fact, this crazy event was a better customer service story than I could have ever made up on my own, so I took the time to write it down while it was all fresh in my mind. The drama that occurred here went on during my stay, but rather than carry this story out much longer, I will say that my departure was just as chaotic as the arrival.

Departure Day

I called down in the morning to verify I had late check out. Although I confirmed it on my arrival, we all know how that turned out. I packed my things in the morning, so I could focus my last few hours on my writing. I was laughing at myself for having a late check out with the noisy freeway still humming loudly, when I would have probably gotten more done at home.

After I finished the chapter I was working on, I called the front desk just to make sure my key would still work since this was a late check out. I spoke to my pal Lydia who assured me everything would be fine. I remember snickering to myself thinking, "I would be willing to make a wager that my key won't work when I come back up the stairs." I even felt a little guilty about my cynicism.

I laughed as I rode the elevator downstairs to pick up that rickety cart that was going to help me get my things back to my vehicle. I moved my car to the front to make loading easier and headed back up the elevator to my room to get my luggage. I got to the door and tried all my tricks to get this door to open but alas… it would not. Forgive me for wondering if Lydia actually might have done this on purpose this time. I choose to believe she didn't, but can this many things really happen when someone competent is handling them?

I had to go to the front desk again and ask for an additional key, explaining that somehow, they didn't work... again. She shrugged her shoulders mentioning the time, as if somehow it was my fault for having a late check out. Even though she had just confirmed five minutes ago that everything would be fine

After several more trips up and down the elevator to get everything into my car, I left **Hotel Hell**, never to return.

The **#BrightSide** to this ridiculous and true story is a sweet housekeeper named Brenda. She was a beacon of light to me—kind, considerate, and eager to please. Brenda, thank you for making me believe that even when a company botches the hiring practices of the entire front-end staff, the back-end staff can make a difference to the people they encounter.

If it's Broke... FIX IT!

Do you think I will EVER recommend this hotel to anyone? Do you think I will share this comedic experience with others to make sure they don't find themselves in the same predicament?

The opportunity cost here is more substantial than an entire week's stay. If I was the manager of this hotel or if I had been training the staff, this is what I would have done.

- Assigned a solidly English-speaking person to be my liaison.
- Made sure that the client had a stellar experience for the rest of the time and had my staff check in regularly.
- Comp'd the stay, asked for a "mystery shopper" evaluation on how I could improve my hotel.
- Offered a free stay again in three or six months to re-evaluate the changes that occurred.

There will be challenges in all businesses. The way they are handled is what defines the type of company you are.

In conclusion, we can see what happens to a business that skips the **Customer Service Carnival.** They turn what should have been an epic **Experience** into a warning story of how not to treat customers. Your goal should be to create **Raving Fan**s, which are your catalysts to the coveted **Rock Star Referrals**.

Chapter 18

RECEIVING ROCK STAR REFERRALS

"In Sales, a referral is the key to the door of resistance."
– Robert Foster Bennett

Now that we are familiar with what NOT to do in Customer Service, we can just reverse the process to come up with a formula for success. When you treat people the way you want to be treated, with dignity and respect, you will find them to be much more willing participants in helping you build your business and your brand.

This chapter is dedicated to helping you learn how to create a **Raving Fan** base that will sing your praises and gladly connect you to their friends, because they are proud to do business with you.

Let's use the previous chapter as a reference point for receiving **Rock Star Referrals**. As a "frequent flyer" at hotels, I am a great brand advocate for establishments that impress me. One of the best examples I've seen of customer service in the hotel industry is my dear friend, Ted Rubin, and his relationship with Ritz Carlton Hotels.

Every time Ted stays at a Ritz Carlton, he posts a picture on **Social Media** of the welcome gift they left in his room, or he acknowledges something they did to impress or delight him. The Ritz has a high commitment to customer satisfaction and are very successful at creating **Raving Fans** like Ted Rubin.

I recognize that every hotel chain doesn't have the budget to provide some of the things the Ritz does, but if you think that a hefty budget is what it is all about, you are completely missing the point. Ted loves the Ritz because they acknowledge and appreciate him as a guest. He loves the Ritz because they listen to him and he knows they care. It isn't the VALUE of the gift; it is the acknowledgement that you matter!

If we review the situation from **Hotel Hell**, they could have redeemed themselves at any time by making a few thoughtful, but minor adjustments.

What if…

- Lydia had apologized for the mix up with the room and offered to buy me a cup of coffee at the restaurant across the parking lot while she made sure the keys worked?
- Someone had brought my luggage up, after they were successful at getting into the room.
- The hotel sent up some extra coffee, water, or even extra toiletries to the room with a quick note apologizing for the inconvenience?
- The staff popped a note under the door that said they know I was busy working on my book, and that if I wanted to eat in my room, someone would run across the parking lot to pick up my food?

I can continue with the possibilities, but I think you get the point. Three of the solutions above cost ZERO dollars. The other one costs a few dollars but are things that **most** hotels provide for free anyway. This is a great example of how a little bit of goodwill could have gone a very long way.

Most people accept apologies and recognize true attempts at making things right. The more things you can do to show people you care, the more likely they are to forgive the challenges. When you stack on unapologetic inconveniences, like layers of a never-ending cake, it is pretty hard to redeem your image in your customers eyes.

Recognizing that it is difficult, I still recommend you work at it. Not just because it is the right thing to do, but also from an entrepreneurial perspective, you should consider the **Lifetime Value (LTV)** of a Customer.

Lifetime Value (LTV)

When talking about Referrals, you need to understand the **LTV (Lifetime Value)** of a Customer. A customer who continues to use your products or services and shares them with others has a value far beyond the "**One & Done**" mentality of the average salesperson.

I don't want to confuse you with the complicated formulas that some companies use to put an actual dollar value on each person; but I **Believe** using myself as an example will clearly show that the financial damage **Hotel Hell** experienced as a result of poor customer service was far greater than this individual visit.

Simple Math

As an author who needs dedicated time to write without distractions, I stay at a hotel four to ten days at a time, four to six times a year. Since we are using simple math, I am going to use a flat $100 as the daily room rate, because it is easy to calculate.

Even using low numbers, here is a very short-term loss of the hotel.

> **LOW END—Personal Business as an Author**
> 4 night's stay x 4 times a year x $100 a night = $1600 a year in revenue
> **$1600 a year x 5 years = $8000**

> **HIGH END—Personal Business as an Author**
> 10 night's stay x 6 times a year x $100 a night = $6000 a year in revenue
> **$6000 a year x 5 years = $30,000**

Now take these numbers and extend them out to ten years by doubling the numbers above. Look at the value then! The loss in revenue from my personal stays during a ten-year period range between $16,000—$60,000 and when you factor in that hotels charge more than $100 a night, the revenue loss will likely reach six figures. This isn't even taking into account the guests that I invite into town, my connections in this community, and my need to rent out meeting facilities or to recommend those facilities to other entrepreneurs.

Now, it gets really scary for the owners of this establishment when you multiply the **LTV** by the number of people who have been frustrated and offended by the treatment they received. Many people will just leave the premises without a word. They will make sure to share the horror story with their family, friends, and business associates. The repercussions of a $2 Toothbrush, endless inconveniences, and having a staff that hasn't been to the **Customer Service Carnival** for training, are so much more detrimental to a business than what you see on the surface.

Reward Behavior You Want Repeated

Earlier in the book, I reminded you to always "Reward behavior you want repeated." Since referrals are something we want repeated, this is an area you should concentrate some energy on.

Most **DS** companies have an incentive program that provides an opportunity for customers to earn free or discounted products. Those programs usually involve quality incentives that you, as the consultant, can purchase for a deeply discounted price. These items are usually given to clients as loyalty gifts, gifts with purchase, and thank you gifts for hosting or providing referrals.

In *DS 201,* we will talk about using them to increase multiple areas of your business. For now, we are going to focus on utilizing them to receive those **Rock Star Referrals** to keep your pipeline full.

Step Up Your Game

People love to share with their friends about the great value and great service they receive. I hope you recognize, those Referrals are not given out to consultants who are sailing in the **Sea of Sameness**. When your level of service impresses others, the word gets around. You will have clients, and even new recruits, who know who you are by reputation.

Providing inexpensive, but often personalized gifts, leaves an incredible impression of understanding and caring. When someone you do business with remembers your name, your birthday, your favorite color, flower or fragrance, it makes you feel special. You naturally want to continue doing business with them and are proud to refer your friends for the same type of treatment.

If you want your clients to feel like you care about them, invest some time and energy getting to know them. The little things can make all the difference in setting yourself apart.

A quote that is most notably attributed to Maya Angelou says it best:

"People will forget what you said,
People will forget what you did,
But people will never forget
How you made them feel." – Maya Angelou

I can tell you, I won't soon forget how the staff at **Hotel Hell** made me feel.

I will NEVER sing their praises, recommend them, or stay at that hotel again. It was clear to me that not only did they not care about me, they were also ill-equipped to handle a simple toothbrush request. Imagine what would have happened in an emergency!

If I had referred you to that hotel, and you received that treatment, it automatically reflects negatively on me as a person. It doesn't mean it is my fault, but my reputation of delivering excellence to others is what provides the expectation of a great recommendation. Your customers are putting their reputations on the line to refer you, so when you WOW them with your service, they will be confident in referring business to you.

Never Say Never

I would like to caution you about using the word NEVER. I used it above to make this specific point, so keep that in mind as you are reading.

Above, I wrote,

"I will NEVER sing their praises, recommend them, or stay at that hotel again."

So, is it true that I would NEVER stay there again? Let's explore some possibilities.

If I received a basket of fruit or flowers at my door from that hotel, with a card that said:

> *Dear Mrs. Fitch,*
>
> *We would like to apologize for the unfortunate circumstances surrounding your recent stay at our hotel. Your comments and suggestions have been acknowledged, and we would love for you to come back and give us another chance to not only supply your needs, but to "WOW" you with our service during your complimentary stay. Your business is important to us, and we would value your input on the new training we have provided for our staff.*
>
> *We appreciate your feedback and we look forward to hearing back from you soon!*

There is something new to consider. Would you go back if you received a gift and a letter like that?

- Acknowledging your feelings.
- Apologizing for the problems.
- Offering to fix it.
- Providing a complimentary way for you to see their improvements in action.

I would go back in a heartbeat. Want to know why?

I **Believe** everyone deserves a second chance. I don't know about you, but I've made some mistakes in my life and I recognize the value of an opportunity. I want to give people a chance to make me feel special and recognized. Imagine the difference in my experience if they welcomed me by name, had extra water and coffee in the room, and made sure to put me on the quietest side of the hotel because they knew I was writing my book.

The simple truth is,

> *"We all just want to be UNDERSTOOD,*
> *ACKNOWLEDGED, and VALUED."*

Now that we know the value of how we make others feel, do you want to know how to get those referrals flowing in? **Believe** it or not, the best way is to ASK.

Get your ASK in Gear

Author and Speaker Debbie Allen, reminds us to **Get your ASK in Gear**. If we want to grow our businesses, we cannot be afraid to ASK for business, ASK for referrals, or ASK for support. The common denominator here is to ASK.

In previous chapters, we have discussed why **FEAR** holds us back. When we **#EvictTheBully** we can conquer many of our old beliefs and surge forward with new strength and **Confidence**. When we remember the **WIIFM** (What's In It For Me?) method and use that to support the request, asking for referrals is easy.

If you watch my daily **Livestreams** or have taken my **FREE 3-Day Mini Course called #RockThatStream**, you know that I teach about how you must ASK for what you want. On each broadcast, I share who I am, provide actionable value they can use to help themselves, and in exchange for that value, I earn the right to ASK for something in return. Some of them are the same requests, others change depending on the day and what the topic is, but I always ASK… IF

- I **ASK** them to share out the broadcast—**IF** they are finding value.
- I **ASK** them to Tweet me on Twitter—**IF** they have additional questions I can answer during the week.
- I **ASK** them to check out my YouTube channel—**IF** they want to see my daily **VLOG**.
- I **ASK** them to join my **Entrepreneurial Rock Stars Facebook Group**—**IF** they want to be around others who want to "Give as much as they get."
- And of course,
- I **ASK** you to go to my website **www.VickiFitch.com/DS101**—**IF** you want additional resources.

The message I am trying to share is that I always get my **ASK** in Gear… **IF** I am providing some type of value to others.

Resolving Pain Points, leads to Referrals

Let's look at a real-life situation that effectively illustrates the point.

You sell a line of all-natural cleaning supplies and have just sold a package to Lucy. She is a friend who has a child with leukemia. She has been feeling overwhelmed about keeping her home as germ-free as possible, recognizing she can't use harsh chemicals. Those substances could cause more harm to her child's fragile system. She is thrilled that you showed her how to clean surfaces using only your products and plain water! She feels renewed strength and **Confidence** that she is providing a safer environment for her child and her family. She is now committed to getting it done as quickly as possible.

Here is how you could respectfully **Get your ASK in Gear:**

> **Lucy:** "Thank you so much for your time today. I feel like this is the solution I've been looking for!"
>
> **You:** "It is my pleasure, Lucy! Providing a clean and safe environment for our families is important. I am so glad I could help! I am sorry that your family is going through this trial and I am honored to assist you. I imagine you have a support group recommended by either the doctor or the hospital that has other families battling the same concerns. If you think this would benefit them as well, would you please share these cards with them?"
>
> **Lucy:** "Of course! Actually, my friend Emily, whom I met at the treatment center, is going through the same thing! We were just talking about it last week."
>
> **You:** "I would love to help Emily and her family. Would you mind making the introduction, so I can do my best to help her family as well?"
>
> **Lucy:** "Yes! I will message her right now. I know this is something that she feels is urgent as well."

I recognize that not all situations will have an urgent nature to them. But the saying "Birds of a feather, flock together." is true. People who are going through similar circumstances have meetings, Facebook Groups, Chat Rooms, etc. that connect them with other people with similar interests or situations. These are often referred to as **Tribes**.

Asking them if they know anyone else that you can serve gives them a chance to think about others in need. Reminding them that you are available and willing to help provides an additional layer of support. Offering them a gift, incentive, or reward becomes the icing on the cake that encourages them to also think outside of that immediate circle. It is a perfect opportunity to develop **Scouts** to really amplify your business.

Please note that there was no "pouncing" going on. The conversation above didn't ask for a list of names of everyone who needs your products or services. It was focused on a specific set of people experiencing a **Pain Point** that you can resolve. Compassion and concern were expressed with the goal of HELPING other people, not serving your own needs or sales goals.

The truth is, Lucy is actually a prime candidate for joining your team. We will discuss a graceful approach to recruiting her and how to effectively engage **Scouts** in much more detail in *DS 201*.

There are a couple other things I want to share with you in this book to support your long-term efforts in this industry, including tapping into the power of **Social Media**.

Chapter 19
KEEP THE SOCIAL IN SOCIAL MEDIA

"The future of business is social."
– Barry Libert

I recognize there are going to be different levels of **Social Media** and **Livestreaming** users, so I've addressed some of the basics to get your business started off on the right path. *DS 301* is dedicated to a more in depth understanding of how to use the major **Social Media** (**SM**) platforms and the best practices for each.

For this chapter, I have focused on Facebook and how to resolve the **Top 4 Biggest Mistakes** the Direct Sales industry makes. At the time of the rewrite of this book, Facebook (**FB**) is the dominant player in the **Social Media** game. It has over 1.5 Billion DAILY active users, so although each platform has different descriptions for engagement, we have primarily used the references of **Liking, Commenting,** and **Sharing**. These are all based on the **FB** platform.

If you have been avoiding getting involved in the **Social Media** space, don't delay any longer. If you want to build your business, you NEED to understand **Social Media**. You must have a **Digital Footprint**.

The purpose of this section is simply to highlight some things to help you move forward on your **Social Media** journey. It will also discuss a few things to avoid, to help keep you out of trouble. I understand that some of you may think you understand **Social Media** and its proper usage. You may be right. However, in my experience, over 90% of the people I speak to (Yes 90%!) don't really understand how to use it properly or effectively. So even if you are a seasoned pro, take a quick read. If nothing else, it will provide you with some reference points to train your team members.

Social Media is... SOCIAL!

One of the first points I want you to understand (and probably the most important) is one of the simplest. Social Media is... SOCIAL!

I know, it is a simple concept. When you think about it, it's even obvious. It is also one of the most overlooked principles in the industry. **Social Media** is supposed to be SOCIAL. When people start forgetting that and start using it exclusively as a marketing tool, they miss the point of the platform, and the opportunity to really connect with the audience through authentic engagement.

"Without engagement, Social Media is a waste of time."

That might sound harsh, but it is true. **Social Media** needs to be SOCIAL to keep us connected to our friends and the brands we love.

More often than we like to admit, it becomes more about the content *provider* rather than the content *consumer*. When that happens, what we produce just becomes noise that people will simply ignore. Your goal as a content creator is to figure out what your audience wants to know and find a fun or unique way to deliver it. That is when your posts are more likely to go **Viral**.

Authentic social connection evokes emotions to be effective. Sometimes we laugh or cry. Sometimes we are inspired or outraged. Sometimes we look at things from a new or unique perspective. In all these instances, we FEEL something.

It reminds me of something Jim Rohn used to say. Although I can't remember the exact quote, it was something like this:

"Make me laugh, make me cry.
Just make me FEEL something." – Jim Rohn

Social Media is like that. We love content that inspires us to FEEL. The more passionately you share the content or the message, the better chance you have of others engaging with you and sharing your content.

There are different emotions, different platforms, different personalities, and different rules. It is just like back in grade school. You have to survey the people and the playground to figure out where you belong.

Social Media Playground

The **Social Media** playground has a lot of different equipment and a lot of different players. To make it more confusing, you will find that some of the participants play by different rules.

Let's outline some of the playground hierarchy.

KNOW IT ALL—The people who never read the rules **ToS** (Terms of Service) or get to know the playground etiquette on what is cool and what isn't. These people either frustrate others or get themselves put in "**Facebook Jail**" (It is a real, yet imaginary place—Ha! Figure that one out!)

ELITISTS—The people who read the rules but figure they don't apply to them. They are somehow "special". Maybe they have a lot of **Friends** or **Followers** who have been "**Liking**" what they do. This confuses them into thinking they should continue with their poor behavior, because they are under the false impression it is working.

RULE FOLLOWERS—These people read the rules and interpret everything in the most conservative way possible. If they don't understand, they will look to someone else in the pecking order and follow their lead. The problem is, if they are following the wrong person, they end up falling off the proverbial monkey bars, bumping their heads, and trying to figure out what happened.

WALLFLOWERS—Some people are afraid to play at all because they don't know the rules. They try to stay off the playground altogether because they might embarrass themselves or do something to irritate one of the **Kingpins** and alienate themselves.

LURKERS—They are a bit like the WALLFLOWERS, but they don't mind getting on the playground to watch what others are doing. They are afraid of participating for **FEAR** of making a **Comment** that will create a problem. Instead, they lurk in **Facebook Groups**, watch what you are posting, view your **Livestreams**, and occasionally, if they feel confident enough, they will quickly hit the "**Thumbs up**" on a post and feel a quick surge of success. (This group has more strength than they realize because they make up a vast majority of the playground. Ironically, they are just too busy trying to make sure they do things right to realize what a powerful force they are!)

LEADERS—These are the people that think they know what they are doing and are well-intentioned. They are trying to build businesses and brands. They feel like they have a good handle on things. Sometimes, they even call themselves experts. The truth is, they have just been learning on the fly from the other Groups on the playground. They have a little better comprehension, but not necessarily a greater understanding, about why what they are doing is working… or not.

SOCIAL MEDIA ROYALTY (The Kingpins)—These are the true leaders in the community. They know the rules and are practicing them. This group knows the ins and outs of the cliques that are on the playground. They work to connect with people by providing value and information to help make the playground a safer, more inviting space to play in. They typically have opportunities for you to participate in free Groups, but are also savvy enough to have paid options. They engage in training and developing the next lineage of royalty to continue keeping the playground safe. These people are revered by others and often asked to speak at **Social Media** conferences. This is because they have valid information to share that benefits the community.

SOCIAL MEDIA MARAUDERS —These people parade around in **SMR (Social Media Royalty)** clothes but are only imitating the truly authentic people. These people can be tricky to spot because they talk the good talk. They may even provide great value. However, they are usually there for selfish reasons and when you run out of money, they run out of time to acknowledge you. (I also refer to these people as **Vultures**.)

Now that you understand the people that are hanging out in the space, I want to cover a few principles to help you understand the basic premise and show you where the Direct Sales industry particularly goes astray.

Biggest Mistakes in Social Media

The 4 biggest mistakes the Direct Selling industry makes in Social Media:

1. Expecting results from **Social Media** without engaging with others.
2. Creating multiple **Profiles** instead of **Pages**.
3. Adding Business content to your **Profile** instead of your **Page**.
4. Adding people to **Facebook Groups** without their permission.

We will address all four of these concerns and provide you some simple solutions to keep you from being forced over to **Fitchslap Island** and maybe getting stuck on **Salesy Shore**.

MISTAKE #1—Expecting Results Without Engaging with Others

Mistake #1 can be easily corrected with Rule #1 in **Social Media**…

Be SOCIAL

As I mentioned before, **Social Media** is...SOCIAL. That means **Liking**, **Commenting**, and **Sharing** to engage with others should be the main reason you are there. You should NOT be there just to sell your products like a hawker does when selling refreshments in the stands at a professional sporting event. You should be developing relationships.

You should engage in RELEVANT content that you actually care about. These are things that align with your values and beliefs. You should **Share** because it means something to you and you **Believe** it will bring value to others. You should NOT **Share** just to gain the attention of someone who has a larger audience than you or because you are hoping that it will go **Viral**.

When you are only there for personal gain and aren't bringing value to the community, others will see through your thinly veiled disguise. If you are using **Vanity Metrics** to gauge your importance, you are acting as one of the **Mini Marauders** who falsely **Believe** that numbers are a true measurement of their personal value. You shouldn't worry about the number of **Followers** you have or the number of **Likes** you receive. They are not as relevant as your engagement. Focus on that and your **SM** following will grow.

MISTAKE #2—Creating Multiple Profiles

Having multiple **Profiles** violates Facebook's **ToS** (Terms of Service), which means you could temporarily or permanently lose access to your account. In order to understand this error, you may need a clearer understanding of some industry terms.

Profiles, Pages & Groups

Most people confuse a **Profile** with a **Page,** so I've outlined the basics below to assist you. Understanding these simple distinctions will alleviate some challenges on the platform.

> **Facebook Profile**—Referred to as your **Profile**—This is your personal page. According to Facebook's **ToS**, every individual can only have ONE **Profile**.

Facebook Page—Referred to as your **Page or Business Page**—For those of you who have been around **Social Media** for a while, it used to be commonly called a **Fan Page**. This can be for a business, a brand, a band, a public figure, etc. You can have as many **Pages** as you like, but they must all be attached to a **Profile**.

Facebook Group—A Group can be made or joined. At the time of this publication, there are 3 different types—Secret, Closed or Public. (Most of the time, I recommend Closed for some very specific reasons, which I discuss in *DS 301*.)

If you are starting your first business, it stands to reason that you wouldn't understand what to do. When you originally came on the platform, there was a button that said, "Create Account" so you repeat what you already know and make another account for your business.

For example, Sally Social creates a **Profile** to get started on Facebook. When she starts her business, she mimics what she has seen, or thinks she has seen others do. Instead of creating a **Page** for her business, she creates another **Profile** called Sally Social XYZ. Since each individual is only allowed to have ONE **Profile**, she is in violation of Facebook's current **ToS**. This can get her put in **Facebook Jail** or have her account banned altogether.

This **FEAR** is what keeps a lot of new participants from using **Social Media** and one of the reasons that *DS 301* is an entire in-depth book focused on the details of how to effectively use **Social Media** and **Livestreaming.**

MISTAKE #3—Adding Business Content to Your Personal Profile

Many people in the **DS** industry have not received adequate, if any, training on how to properly use **SM** to market their businesses. You have probably been frustrated more than once by someone who gets into the industry and then floods their **Newsfeed** with:

- Sale Brochures or Flyers
- Recruiting Information

- Specials they are having right now.
- Headlines that say:
  - o "Buy this!"
  - o "Join me!"
  - o "Make Money Now!"

Those are **Business Page** posts. (Not ones I recommend either!) There are fesw things that get people's posts blocked on their **Newsfeed** as quickly as an overzealous person in the **DS** industry.

Think of it this way. Facebook is trying to provide a safe and inviting environment for their users, who are primarily there to connect with their friends. **Newsfeeds** shouldn't become a constant scrolling advertisement. When we have an interest in products and services, we can **Like** a company's **Business Page** to receive information from them. Clicking that button is basically an invitation for their content to show up in your **Newsfeed**. If they didn't have these parameters set up, you would have less control and a much different experience when you logged in to your account.

When you keep that concept in mind, it is easier to determine what you should and should not post on your **Profile**. Your **Friends** are counting on you to post things that are interesting to them and to share updates about your life. Accepting a **Friend** request, unless you modify the defaults or group your **Friends** into categories, means their content can end up in your **Newsfeed**. When someone extends or accepts a **Friend** request, it shows they trust you and the content you are posting. When that trust is abused, they will likely block you or your content.

The idea of keeping personal and business content separate appeals to us, but most of us want our family and friends to know what we are doing. We want to share our success and our opportunity with everyone we know, in the hopes that those that are interested will contact us. Some feel **FEAR** of the **Naysayers** that will try to discourage them and the internal conflict… *to share or not to share…* can really weigh us down. We know if we don't share, we will be disappointed if our friends get involved with our company… but not with us. I am hoping that your **Confidence** in your business is growing with each page of this book and your **Confidence** in **Social Media** is growing with each page of this chapter.

There is a way to creatively share this information on both platforms while still abiding by the rules of the playground. I call this **Blending** and have included all the details in *DS 301*. In addition, I added in a part that will help you understand the basics of algorithms (to make sure your **Friends** are seeing your content) in a simple and fun way to keep you entertained!

MISTAKE #4—Adding People to Facebook Groups Without Permission

I know this is going to be a sore subject for some of you and I'm sorry to be the bearer of bad news. This is a major faux pas in the **Social Media** space. Even if someone you trust is encouraging this, please let me educate you by sharing that this is not good etiquette. It is considered both rude and disrespectful.

If you want to invite people to a **FB Group**, show them respect by allowing them the option of joining or declining your invitation. When you send a personal invitation, you are more likely to gain members who actually want to be part of your Group. That will create more engagement and build the quality relationships you are seeking.

Most people who add others to a Group without permission are doing so in order to try to build big numbers. They see the number as a sort of "popularity contest". They are under the misconception that the bigger the Group, the better. That simply isn't true. The number of members is a **Vanity Metric.** You should be more concerned with the **quality** of the people in the Group, not the quantity of people who have joined. I would rather have a Group of 10 active and engaged members than a Group of 10,000 **Lurkers.**

NOTE: If you are involved in a company that is encouraging you to add people into a **Facebook Group** without permission, give them the benefit of the doubt and remember that they are learning too. Recommend they connect with me directly. I will provide a consultation to help them set up **Social Media** practices that will help you and your team grow without getting a poor reputation in the industry. (If your company needs some reputation management, I can help with that too. Send them to my website or let me know who I need to speak with and we will try to provide the assistance your organization needs.)

The primary objectives of a **Facebook Group** are building relationships, finding common interests and providing value to a Group of like-minded individuals. As entrepreneurs, it is valuable to have access to others who will give you an honest opinion of a program, a logo, an idea or a decision. We often beta test programs through each other and provide genuine feedback. The insight of others who care about you is an incredible resource.

My motivation in starting my Group was to find qualified entrepreneurs, in all areas of expertise, whom I could confidently refer to my clients. I wanted to build a community of trusted professionals who I had personally vetted myself or who were highly recommended by other trusted friends.

I typically invite individual people that I think will add value to the community to join. I do this not because I want the biggest Group, but because I want the BEST. There are many Groups out there that become a "free for all", where everyone is posting their company's latest flyer or trying to recruit all the Group members to their organizations or even into their own **Facebook Groups**. Some of them get so distracted with their complaints and negativity that they wallow in their difficulties and look for others to commiserate with them. I highly recommend you look for a Group of people who will help you look at the **#BrightSide** of things and who will try to provide value to you and the other members.

In the **Entrepreneurial Rock Stars (ERS)**, we provide daily threads to create interaction and to encourage connection. The guidelines are strictly enforced but are set up to prevent the **Social Media Marauders** from invading the Group. Everyone has a chance to share what they do and offer information or services to others in a structured way. This prevents the **Know it All's** and the **Elitists** from hijacking the Group's wall and inundating people with their "Buy Now!" or "Check out this opportunity!" noise.

> *"Facebook Groups*
> *aren't a place to sell your products or recruit people.*
> *They are a place to provide value and build relationships."*

That doesn't mean that you won't end up with clients from your Group. It means that it shouldn't be your primary focus. There are courses being sold and "leaders" suggesting that growing a huge **Facebook Group** is like planting your own personal money tree. I personally find that offensive and I hope if you have heard that before, you will recognize that it is a short-sighted perspective. That philosophy is more likely to sink your ship than to be the wind filling your sails as you head over to **Success Island**.

If you decide to start a Group, I highly recommend you read *DS 301* so you can set yourself and your members up for success. It is imperative you have rules and guidelines from the start to provide clarity and prevent confusion. Managing a **Facebook Group** takes time and energy, so make sure it is something you will enjoy and are willing to commit to doing.

Since we are talking about **Facebook Groups**, I would be remiss if I didn't invite you to join the **Entrepreneurial Rock Stars**. The requirements to participate are simple. We are looking for entrepreneurs who want to give at least as much as they get.

Consider this my personal invitation to you since we may not have met yet. If you think you would **Vibe with my Tribe**, we would love to have you. There is a direct link available at **www.VickiFitch.com/DS101**.

Now that I've given you the basics of **Social Media**, it is time to talk about my favorite way to connect… **Livestreaming**.

Chapter 20

LEVERAGING THE POWER
OF LIVESTREAMING

"Livestreaming is a great way to build community,
storytell and engage with others in real time."
– Kim Garst

am keeping this chapter short because I have an entire video course you can watch and some additional books that will provide details on how to truly capitalize on this rapidly growing opportunity. **For access to #RockThatStream,** my **FREE 3-Day Mini Course,** go to **www.VickiFitch.com/DS101**.

If you aren't currently **Livestreaming,** you are missing out on a potential gold mine of opportunity. (You may see it written as Live Streaming, but I personally consider it a verb. The act of streaming live, so I added it as a **Fitchism** to keep any of you 'grammar fanatics' from sending me a sternly worded letter. LOL)

As I mentioned, the **KLT Factor** increases exponentially when people can see you, hear your message, and watch your delivery style. I have met some of the most amazing people, secured speaking engagements, added clients in six different countries, and built two successful podcasts all due to **Livestreaming**.

My first experience with **Livestreaming** was Periscope—Twitter's **Livestreaming** app. I started broadcasting daily with my tagline: "*Sales to Social Media and Everything in Between.*" I quickly gained a following. I delivered value every day and started offering a free 20-minute consultation to my viewers. Having potential clients fill out a questionnaire, doing some research, and showing them that I could help their businesses was easy. In the first five months, I had done over $50,000 in sales. Not bad for clicking a "Start Broadcast" button and sharing knowledge that was already in my head.

My influence and experience in this space has grown significantly. I developed a presentation called "$40K in 4 Weeks" and then after I had done over $100K in sales in the first quarter of 2017, I created a signature talk called **Leveraging the Power of Livestreaming: Converting Contacts to Cash**. You can see how the momentum built and how it can benefit your business and your brand.

My point here is not that I am special, but that all of us possess knowledge that is valuable to someone else. This is knowledge that we typically take for granted and assume everyone knows. Yours might be how to braid your daughter's hair or how to save the most money couponing. It doesn't matter what your skill is. **Livestreaming** is a way to deliver your content worldwide, instantly. That can lead to a **Tribe** of people who may recommend you to others or may want to purchase your products or services.

If you think there is nothing to **Livestream** in your business, I would venture to guess I could come up with something interesting. And if I can… you can too. Anytime you can add a visual element to your teaching or instruction, it will create a stronger impact.

Here are some examples of topics that include a visual element to them:

1. **Essential Oils**—Explaining how to reduce headaches, inflammation, or health problems with special oil combinations. Showing the actual application sites and the best method to apply it. Answering questions at the same time will increase the audience's **Confidence** in your expertise, which will increase your **KLT Factor**.

2. **Jewelry**—Demonstrating how to layer different pieces of jewelry to create stunning looks or to show how you can look slimmer or taller

depending on your jewelry selections. Discussing necklines and which pieces best accentuate the different styles.

3. **Clothing**—Identifying body types and the best style of clothes to accentuate your most favorable features. Demonstrating scarf tying and the numerous ways you can use a single piece to accessorize your outfit and highlight those favorite features.

4. **Animal Trainers**- How-To broadcasts demonstrating the proper way to brush an animal's teeth, give positive reinforcement training, clean hooves, or brush or braid the animal's hair or mane. Answer questions as well and you can become their animal **Expert**.

5. **Illustrators, Artists, Bakers or Crafters** (Overhead Demonstrations)— You may start with the broadcast facing you before switching directions (with the right piece of inexpensive equipment) and showing how to draw, mix, create, or perform a specific task or activity. There is a huge market for YouTube video tutorials, but LIVE tutorials where people can ask questions are in huge demand! Some of what you demonstrate can actually be sold while you are on the air!

NOTE: The right equipment is important. You can get a **discount** on my recommended items by going to **www.VickiFitch.com/DS101.** The link and details for the discount are there.

The possibilities are endless. I have worked with many different **DS** companies as well as with Doctors, Lawyers, Dentists, Real Estate Agents, Mortgage Brokers, Financial Planners, Retailers, Schools and numerous other professions and businesses. It is important to recognize there is something you know that others don't understand. Together, we can find a way to deliver your message to the marketplace.

At the time of writing this book, I do daily simultaneous broadcasts on both Periscope & FB Live at 6pm Pacific, delivering value on "Everything Entrepreneur." I also have a daily **VLOG** on YouTube, which outlines my #12Books12Months journey. I have created a strong following, secured many clients, and have been asked to speak around the world because I am willing and able to provide content in a live format. I encourage you to add **Livestreaming** to your marketing efforts, so you can capitalize on one of the hottest **Social Media** trends.

This chapter is designed to give you a vision of what **Livestreaming** can do without inundating you. *DS 301* and **#RockThatStream** will elaborate on the details, so here is a list of my Top Tips to increase your audience, build your brand, expand your influence, and improve your sales.

1. **Be Consistent**—Have a daily schedule if possible. If you pick an actual time, some people will put it on their calendar. If you can't pick a time, you can set an expectation that you will be on every day, or every Wednesday, etc. If having a specific time doesn't work for you, continue to broadcast whenever you can. Just recognize that the more consistent you can be, the more your **Followers** will connect with you.

2. **Have a CTA (Call to Action)**—Every broadcast should include a **CTA**. Be prepared to send your viewers to your website or a landing page. Gathering email addresses so you can continue to provide value is an important part of growing your business.

3. **Pick Your Topic in Advance**—Decide what you want to talk about and use that in the title and on any reminders to entice viewers. You can also include a Q & A section to add depth.

4. **Send Reminders**—I send out a "**Live in 5**" infographic across my **Social Media** platforms before I start a broadcast to remind my **Friends** and **Followers** that it is time to join me. This gives them a heads up that I am going live, and provides them the opportunity to share it out with their friends as well.

5. **Look Professional**—Professional doesn't mean you must be dressed up and made up. It means to be prepared. If you are going to use props, materials, or notecards, have them ready in advance. Find a location that is presentable and free from unnecessary noise and distractions.

6. **Camera Angle**—Try to have your camera at eye level so it appears that you are looking into their eyes. It has been said that when you are looking down at people, it makes them feel inferior. This often makes them feel

you are less trustworthy (It is not a true indicator of your sincerity, but many studies have suggested this hurts credibility anyway.)

7. **Deliver Value**—Make the broadcast about the viewers. What value can you provide for them? (Remember the **WIIFM** Method.)

8. **Greet Your Viewers**—This is a personal choice. (I discuss this more in the **#RockThatStream** Mini Course) I am a firm believer in the "Cheers" philosophy. For those of you familiar with the old show, the song says... *"You want to go where everybody knows your name... and they're always glad you came."* That is what I **Believe**, and what I love, when I pop into other people's broadcasts. I like to be recognized and I love recognizing others. It creates camaraderie and helps build your **Tribe**.

9. **Start Your Broadcast Right Away**—Greet your viewers and then dive into your content. Don't "wait" for more people to jump on. (Certainly, never say that either. It is a huge insult to people who come into your broadcast just to hear you say, *"OK we are going to wait until more people show up."* That is disrespectful to the time of the people who showed up when you started. The other people can always catch the beginning on the replay.)

10. **Ask Your Viewers to SHARE**—It is OK to remind your viewers what you would like them to do. (**Get your ASK in Gear.**) For example, I always say, *"Welcome to the broadcast, I appreciate you being here! If you are one of my regular **Followers**, you know you are going to get some tremendous value, so please **Share** this out! If you are new to the broadcast, please put your name in the chat box* (if you are on a platform like Periscope where it is handle related vs. name), *so I can give you a shout-out. Then, feel free to kick back and relax. If the message resonates with you or you are finding value, then please Share it out so we can help as many people as possible."*

11. **Don't Worry About Your Numbers!**—Yes, we want to remind people to **Share** because they get busy and sometimes they don't even think about **Sharing** when listening to a broadcast. The reminder is actually helpful. However, **don't worry about the numbers!** If the broadcast says 0 people are present, speak like you are doing a podcast that people

are going to watch/hear later… because they are! Many of my broadcasts have A LOT more replay than live viewers. Your viewership will grow, and you will get better, so never worry about the numbers. In most platforms, you can't actually tell how many people are watching, because only the ones who are interacting on the app natively show up in the viewer count. Just remember, someone out there needs to hear what you have to say. Your job is to deliver the value!

12. **Answer Questions**—If you are comfortable, I recommend you try to answer live questions. That is one of the huge advantages to watching a live broadcast vs. a recording. It really increases the **KLT Factor** when people feel open enough to ask you questions. I always try to leave time at the end for specific questions that may or may not be about the topic at hand. They may want to ask me about yesterday's broadcast or something else that is in my wheelhouse. If I can't answer it then, I can use that question for tomorrow's topic or add it to my list of future topics. This is valuable feedback about what your audience wants to hear.

13. **Don't be Afraid of Trolls**—A few people may pop into your broadcasts and make off-handed, strange, or even inappropriate comments. Don't worry about them. They are insecure people looking for someone they can fluster. (I do a deep dive into **#TrollPatrol** in *DS 301* and in the **#RockThatStream Livestreaming** course)

14. **Follow Up**—Reply to your **Comments** and **Shares** after the broadcast. The participants will appreciate your connection and it will help build your relevance with the algorithm. We talk more about **AL** and this follow up process in *DS 301*.

I know from speaking around the world about this topic that **Livestreaming** makes most people feel vulnerable. I know from experience that most people tend to avoid vulnerability like the plague. I want you to know that although this is a very comfortable place for me, I do understand why it would cause you to feel a bit hesitant. That is why I created the **#RockThatStream Free 3-Day Mini Course** with step-by-step instructions to get you started off the right way.

For a little extra support, be sure to join the **Entrepreneurial Rock Stars,** then take a deep breath, and hit the Start Broadcast button. We must face our **FEAR** if we want to grow.

Your **Dreams** are depending on you… maybe more than you realize.

Chapter 21

BECOMING A DREAM BUILDER

"If you don't build your Dream,
someone will hire you to help build theirs."
– Tony Gaskins

B uilding your **Dreams** is difficult work.
Believing in yourself when others don't, staying encouraged when you feel like giving up, and moving through the bad days while trying to remember that good days will follow soon enough... is HARD.

Anyone who tells you it isn't is either lying, hasn't been through it, or has forgotten the experience. What I want you to remember is that EVERYTHING is easier when you are not alone. That is what this book was written for—to help you, guide you, and remind you that You Are Not Alone! #YANA

This #12Books12Months series is your resource to becoming the victorious **Dream Builder** inside you. But first, you must understand where you are vulnerable.

*Imagine for a moment that in your arms you are holding a tiny **Baby**. It is a precious child that needs constant care. It was born prematurely, and many said it wouldn't make it. It barely has the strength to cry. When it gets scared, it lets out a quiet little whimper. You gently rock it back and forth, speaking soothing words of comfort until you have lulled this gem back to sleep.*

When your arms start to feel tired, you sit down, prop your arms up, and find a pillow to support the weight. You watch it closely to be sure it is still breathing. You are proud of the care you are providing and the obvious confidence this little one has in you. Nothing will harm this infant while you are watching. You will tirelessly care for this helpless creature and will do whatever it takes to keep this precious bundle safe.

*When it is time for a feeding, you ever so gently walk over to the pantry, set the carrier down, and gather the food to nourish it. You turn off the light, walk out of the closet, and quietly close the door. The **Baby**, who isn't fussing or insisting on being fed, is left inside the closet to starve to death…*

For those of you who are ready to throw this book across the room or yell at me, let me apologize for capturing you in an all too real scenario. I know that being immersed in something as captivating and emotional as parenting can create strong reactions, but I honestly needed you to experience it, because that is exactly what you are doing… to your **Dreams**.

Are your DREAMS dying a Slow Painful Death?

That is actually the title of one of the emails I send in a series after people do a twenty-minute consultation with me.

Why?

Because our **Dreams** are one of our most valuable and precious assets. All too often, when we are most susceptible and they need us to protect them the most, we tuck them in a closet and walk away, never to return. We allow our **Dreams** to die by **SPD (Slow Painful Death)**. We literally STARVE them to death.

With no love, light, positive reinforcement, confirmation, or attention, our **Dreams** will die. They are vulnerable, and they need us.

They need us to **Believe** in them.

They need us to fight for them.

They need us to feed them, nurture them, and protect them!

Are you guilty of committing Dreamicide?

If you deliberately, or through negligence, kill your **Dreams**, that is a crime against yourself. Although, you can't currently be convicted for committing **Dreamicide**, I recommend you take a trip over to **Hope Island** where the *#HopeDealer* will help you resuscitate your barely breathing **Baby** with new life. If you *remember* your **Dreams**, they are still alive, and you can revive them, so they can thrive!

Your Dreams need to see light—Share them with others.

Your Dreams need to be nurtured—Invest in yourself and plan to achieve them.

Your Dreams need to be cherished—Ignore people who mock or scoff at them.

Your Dreams need to be protected—Run off the **Naysayers** who sling mud at them.

Your Dreams need to be fed—Create a **Dream Board** and an action list to accomplish them.

Your Dreams need to be supported—Find a **Tribe** of others who **Believe** in you and are willing to help keep a watchful eye on you and your **Dreams**!

Dream Builders are a **Tribe** of strong warriors. We fight the good fight and recognize that healthy relationships with like-minded people are what help our

Dreams thrive instead of just survive. Although five of the books in this series are dedicated to the Direct Sales Industry, they are truly just **Stepping Stones** on the map to get you to the place where your **Dreams** can grow. The rest of the books are a support system for you to become the best version of yourself no matter what you choose to do.

Do yourself a favor and don't stop with *Direct Selling 101*. **Believe** in yourself and learn to increase your Sales and Leadership skills while you #RockThatTeam in *Direct Selling 201*. Learn how to be a **Social Media** Superstar and #RockThatStream in *Direct Selling 301*. Build your Business & your Brand by Marketing yourself effectively to *#RockThatScene* in *Direct Selling 401* and Step Up to the Big Money using Automation, Affiliation & Offloading and *#RockThatMachine* to a six-figure income and beyond in *Direct Selling 501*.

If you have been hiding behind your **FEAR**, it is time for you to *Evict the Bully in Your Head*, *OWN IT! Step Up & Stand Out*, and maybe even get *#Fitchslapped*. There is *Profit in the Pain* you've been feeling and the *#HopeDealer* is here to encourage you. If your finances are challenged, it's OK. *You're Broke, Not Broken*, and I am going to show you how to *#RockThatDream*.

It is time for you to **Believe** in yourself and your **Dreams** like I do. It is time to embrace **Belief** and the **Confidence** that, You CAN Do It! #YCDI

If you are ready to be a **Dream Builder**, it is time for you to set sail for **Success Island**. On the way, we are going to be stopping by another Island in **Fitchipelago,** so we can *Evict the Bully in Your Head.* We want to make sure they have no power to hold your **Dreams** hostage, or to influence you to leave your **Dreams** stranded somewhere.

Belief takes time and I know that the **Bully in Your Head** wants you to settle for less than your potential. I **Believe** in you and want you to reach **#RockThatDream** Ridge. If you haven't gotten your copy of book number 2 in the series, *Evict the Bully in Your Head*, do yourself a favor and order it today. I put my heart and soul into that book to provide you the step-by-step instructions to kicking your **Bully** to the curb and reclaiming your full potential.

I hope you are reading books every day to help you grow. I hope you are cleaning off that **Dirty Filter** every day to help you see clearly. I also hope you are watching my daily **Livestreams** to help keep you focused, encouraged, and hopeful. The best way I know how to provide that is to sign off with my personal mantra every time. This mantra is what has gotten me to the level of success I've achieved and will continue to help me grow even more…

Dream it,

    Believe it,

        Achieve it!

          #RockThatDream

Check out all the FREE RESOURCES for the book at www.VickiFitch.com/DS101

Appendix

FITCHTIONARY

#12Books12Months	My personal hashtag to brand and identify my **BHAG** to write 12 Books in 12 Months.
#BHAG	A **B**ig **H**airy **A**udacious **G**oal. A goal that scares you and will make you stretch. If you know you can achieve it… it isn't a #BHAG
#Boom	Similar to a **#TruthBomb** A proverbial mic drop that means the content was right on the money and it landed with a loud affirmative thud.
#BrightSide	My hashtag for identifying a situation where the **Bright Side** was recognized or should be recognized. It signifies a choice to find the best in situations. It is also used when people play the **Bright Side** game.
#EvictTheBully	My hashtag for acknowledging the active participation needed to **Evict the Bully in Your Head**. It is also a reminder to focus on the power of choosing to **Believe** in yourself and others.

#Fitch5000	The amazing core group of people supporting me on my **#BHAG** of **#12Books12Months**. Thanks to Doug Crowe for giving vision to that!
#HopeDealer	A nickname my clients gave me because "working with me is like a drug" and that drug is **Hope**. It is also the name of a book in the **#12Books12Months** series.
#IAmEnough	My hashtag for you to remind yourself that **#YouAreEnough** just the way you are.
#JoinTheJourney	My hashtag to encourage others to join the **#12Books12Months** journey. This journey includes becoming the best version of themselves.
#JustSayin	A quippy reminder that the previous statement was a fact or a **#TruthBomb**.
#MadeMyMove	A hashtag for you to share your "Move" with me.
#MakeYourMove	A hashtag to identify when you know you need to "Change your State" or change your state of mind.
#PUYB	The hashtag to remind you to **Pull Up Your Bootstraps**. Something challenging is coming or is about to be said.
#QYF	A Twitter sized version of **Quit Your Fitchin'**. Used to remind people to stop complaining.
#RedIsAlwaysRight	A hashtag that was generated from my podcast, **He Said, Red Said**.
#RockThatDream	My personal branded hashtag and the methodology I apply toward all I do in business and life. My mission is to help others embrace who they are, so they can truly **#RockThatDream**. Rita Esther is credited with that inspiration! It is also the title of one of the **#12Books12Months** series.

#RockThatDream Ridge	The highest point on **Success Island,** which includes a 360-degree view of all of **Fitchipelago**. It is the home to the coveted **Pinnacle of Peace**, where entrepreneurial **Dreams** live.
#RockThatStream	A crystal-clear stream running between **#RockThatDream Ridge** and the **Pain of Perfectionism Peaks**. It is also the sister hashtag of **#RockThatDream** and my signature step-by-step course to teach you how to **Leverage the Power of Livestreaming: Converting Contacts to Cash.**
#TruthBomb	My favorite expression when something is right on the money. This term is especially relevant when the information provided is possibly unwanted, but necessary. A **#TruthBomb** at times, can be synonymous with a **#Fitchslap**.
#YANA	A Twitter Sized version of **#YouAreNotAlone**.
#YCDI	A Twitter Sized version of **#YouCanDoIt**.
#YouAreEnough	A reminder that **#YouAreEnough** just the way you are. It is also part of a global campaign that I am launching with the **#12Books12Months** series.
15 Minute Focus	A **Market Separator** in the scrapbooking industry that solved multiple **Pain Points**. It can also be used to describe 15-Minute blocks of time used to focus on something specific.
Acceptance	A character in *Evict the Bully in Your Head.*
Achieve It Ave	A thoroughfare on **Success Island**.
Addiction	A character in *Evict the Bully in Your Head.*
AL	A friend at Facebook that is the keeper of all information. We talk more about him in future books.
Alcoholism	A character in *Evict the Bully in Your Head.*
Anxiety	A character in *Evict the Bully in Your Head.*
Archipelago	A chain or grouping of islands. See **Fitchipelago**.

Auto Pilot	The conductor of the **Habit Train** and one of the best ways to accomplish more in your life and business.
Baby	A term I use to reference your **Dreams**. It is there to help you recognize that **Dreams** are as precious and vulnerable as an actual baby, and therefore must be cared for and nurtured.
Back to Back	Events that are held consecutively to save time and energy.
Backpeddling	The act of "moving backwards" or withdrawing a question, suggestion or request, usually due to **FEAR.**
Barter Blvd	A route on **Success Island** that often detours people who are afraid to travel on **Sales Street.**
Be Back	A **Be Back** in sales is when someone you are trying to close a transaction with says they will "Be Back". You may also hear things like, "I'll get back to you.", when you are trying to schedule an appointment. It is always best to find a way to finish your business while you have their attention. Most **Be Backs**, never make it back.
Belief	A character in ***Evict the Bully in Your Head.***
Believe	One of the most powerful words in the world. It is the catalyst to most achievement, and the word I emphasize the strongest in my mantra.
Believe it Blvd	A thoroughfare on **Success Island.**
Blend, Blends, Blending	**Blending** is a way to combine business and personal posts to gain maximum exposure without violating Facebook **ToS**. It helps keep you out of "**Facebook Jail**".
BM2OEN	**Buy Me 2 Of Everything New**—My Mantra as a customer in the Direct Sales industry and your target audience!

Bright Side	A game I play with my family, team, and clients to remind everyone that you can find a **Bright Side** in any situation, no matter how frustrating, disappointing or overwhelming it is. **Bright Side** can be ANY idea from the **Obvious to the Outlandish**. The object is to THINK about a positive or funny way to look at the situation. It is a BIG help in keeping a **PMA**.
Bully	**Bully** with a capital "B" represents the **Bully in Your Head**. We will talk about this in detail in *Evict the Bully in Your Head*.
Bully Behavior	When you mentally beat yourself up about mistakes, challenges, or difficult situations.
Bully in Your Head	The voice in your head that tries to convince you that you are Not Good Enough, Not Smart Enough, Not Strong Enough, etc. You must start the eviction process immediately, which I will teach you in *Evict the Bully in Your Head*.
Bundle, Bundles, Bundling	A **Bundle** is when you combine your products and/or services together in ways that benefit you and the customer. It is often used as a **Market Separator** and typically increases sales.
Buying Thresholds	A **Buying Threshold** is an imaginary number that a person won't spend on themselves, without either feeling guilty, or consulting another person about their purchase.
BYT (Bite Your Tongue)	**BYT** stands for **Bite Your Tongue** and is used to stop you from **Backpeddling** or filling in the silence that others need to ponder your questions and formulate an answer. It is also used to protect an individual with **TMI Syndrome** from getting a bad reputation by **Gushing** all over other people.

Coast of Consistency	A pristine coastline on the northeast shore of **Success Island.**
Cockiness	A character in *Evict the Bully in Your Head.*
Cold Turkey	An expression that means to stop immediately.
Comment, Commenting	A **Social Media** term that refers to engaging with a post.
Confidence	A character in *Evict the Bully in Your Head.*
Confidence Causeway	The connection from **Stability Shore** on to **Success Island.**
Consistency	The person shoveling the coal (**Momentum**) into the fire on the **Habit Train** to keep it moving, and your best friend in business.
Courage	A character in *Evict the Bully in Your Head.*
Creativity Creek	A place where you can nurture your creativity on **Success Island.**
CTA (Call to Action)	A directive designed to prompt an immediate response from your audience. It is usually done to get them to opt in, make a purchase or engage with you via **Social Media.**
Customer Service Carnival	A Customer Service training ground for entrepreneurs inside the **Entrepreneurial Theme Park** on **Success Island.**
Depths of Discouragement	A dangerous place off the coast of '**Nough Nation** near the **Ocean of Overwhelm.**
Determination	A character in *Evict the Bully in Your Head.*
Digital Footprint	The digital information available about you on the internet, including your website and **Social Media.**
Dirty Filter	A **Dirty Filter** is one that has been tainted by negative influences and is often a cause of conflict with others.
Doubt	A character in *Evict the Bully in Your Head.*
Downline	The person being sponsored or brought into the company by an **Upline.**

Dream Board	An easy way to keep your **Dreams** alive and in front of you. It is also an excellent way to identify your family's desires, so you can help them achieve their **Dreams** too.
Dream Builder	A person who is committed to the consistent effort of building their own **Dreams** and helping others to build theirs too.
Dream it Drive	A thoroughfare on **Success Island**.
Dream it, **Believe it**, Achieve it	My personal mantra and the way I end my **Livestreams**. Emphasis on **Believe it**.
Dream it, Believe it, Achieve it Bridge	The primary path to get off **Fitchslap Island** and onto **Success Island**.
Dream, Dreams	Your **Dream** is something you intensely desire but have often tucked away in a closet to die via **SPD**. Many people have forgotten to **Dream** or have lost their ability to **Believe** in the possibility that they can come true. That is what the **#12Books12Months** series is about. Helping you boldly claim your **Dreams** while developing an execution strategy to reach them.
Dreamicide	**Dreamicide** is the death of your **Dreams** caused by YOU, either by letting them die via **SPD**, allowing others to pick them apart, or allowing the **Bully in Your Head** to influence you to ignore them. **"Leaving the Baby in the closet."** is committing **Dreamicide**. **#NoDreamicide**
Dreaming into Achieving	The name of the first course I created to help my team learn to **Dream it, Believe it, & Achieve it!**
Drive	A character in ***Evict the Bully in Your Head***.
DS	Short for Direct Sales.

DSA	**DSA** stands for **D**irect **S**ales **A**ssociation, which is an organization that most Direct Sales Companies are members of.
DSA Hopper	A person who jumps from one Direct Sales company to another, never taking the time to become an **Expert**, create a **Market Separator,** or develop long term relationships with clients or team members.
Edutain	The act of **Edu**cating and Enter**tain**ing at the same time, often with laughter.
Efficiency	A railcar on the **Habit Train**.
Empathy	A character in *Evict the Bully in Your Head*.
Entrepreneurial Rock Star	A member of my Facebook Group, the **Entrepreneurial Rock Stars** (**ERS**). Or someone who is crushing it in their space.
Entrepreneurial Theme Park	A place on **Success Island** where we learn about being an entrepreneur.
ERS	The abbreviation for my Facebook Group, the **Entrepreneurial Rock Stars**, which is a Group of entrepreneurs who want to *give* at least as much as they *get*.
Evidence	Items that associate you with your company, business or brand for the purpose of the **Evidence Check**.
Evidence Check	The practice of having a minimum of 5 pieces of **Evidence** on you at all times. Based on the question, "If you were arrested for being a part of your company… would there be enough **Evidence** to convict you?"
Expect the Yes!	Not to be confused with having the **Expectation** that the client is going to purchase, this means to be prepared for the "Yes". Having your paperwork, links, or products ready to go shows your professionalism.
Expectation	Wanting or needing something in return.

Experience	Creating an above average situation, feeling, or event through personal touches, which often involve multiple senses and/or emotions.
Expert	A person who has a comprehensive and authoritative knowledge of or skill in a particular area. Your goal as an entrepreneur should be to become an **Expert** in your field.
Facebook Jail	A real, yet imaginary place, where people who violate the Facebook **ToS (Terms of Service)** go to await judgement on whether they will be let back in the Facebook realm or not. You can be banned from Groups, from posting for a period of time, or from all of Facebook. This is a scary place to be and one of the most important reasons you NEED to connect with people off **Social Media** platforms as well.
Fail	A word the **Bully in Your Head** will try to manipulate you with. **Fail** is a 4-Letter "F" Word and only shows up in this dictionary as a reminder to **#EvictTheBully**. See **Stepping Stones.**
Family Fund	The special fund used for family activities or **Dreams** that helps to keep your family on board your entrepreneurial bus.
Family Night	A special night each week set aside for family time.
Fans	Someone who is a **Fan** of your content, product, or service.
FBN	**FBN** stands for Fictitious **B**usiness **N**ame and it represents the name in which you do business under.
FEAR	A character in *Evict the Bully in Your Head.*
Fear of Rejection Road	A rarely traveled road on **Success Island** that leads to the fastest route to **#RockThatDream** Ridge.

Filter	**Filters** are created by our life experiences and relationships and they are intensified, both positively and negatively, by our self-esteem.
First Call Close	To make the sale the first time you meet with the customer.
Fitch Philosophy	The **Fitch Philosophy** is my perspective on life. It is choosing to look at the **Bright Side**, handling people and problems with **Dignity** and **Grace**, while assuming the best in others. It also focuses on **Empathy** and on actively seeking to understand other people's circumstances. This Philosophy keeps you focused on the positive and helps you to grow as an individual and as an entrepreneur.
Fitchipelago	The chain of islands (see **Archipelago**) located in the **M3 (Money, Mindset & Motivation) Triangle**. The Islands include **Success Island, Hope Island, 'Nough Nation** and **Fitchslap Island.**
Fitchisms	My unique and colorful way of describing things to help you prepare for, understand, and execute things in a fun and progressive way.
Fitchslap	The act of correcting behavior. The **Fitchslap** is a public service. It only comes out when necessary, is always done in **Love**, and is used to redirect the course of someone who has gone astray. It is sometimes necessary to self-inflict a **#Fitchslap** to get you back on course, find the **Bright Side** or help you **Quit Your Fitchin'.**
Fitchslap Island	An island in **Fitchipelago** that you will be visiting during the **#12Books12Months** series.

FitchTap	A **FitchTap** is a gentler reminder of a needed correction in behavior. These are sometimes administered in place of the **Fitchslap** to individuals who are new to the **Fitch Philosophy**, are experiencing some emotional or challenging situation but still need gentle correction, or are going in the right direction but need a gentle **Nudge** to get back on track.
Follow	The act of someone choosing to connect themselves with you on **Social Media**.
Follow Up	The rarely used art of providing Customer Service and a documented way of exponentially increasing sales.
Follow Up Ferry	A rarely used mode of transportation throughout **Fitchipelago**.
Followers	The people who follow you, your content or your **Social Media** profiles.
FOMO	**FOMO** is the **Fear Of Missing Out**. It can often cause us to make decisions that aren't in our best interests.
FRANK	**FRANK** is your new best friend in the Direct Sales Industry. He is an acronym for Friends, **R**elatives, **A**cquaintances, **N**eighbors, **K**ids.
Friend, Friends, Friending	A **Social Media** term on Facebook that refers to people you have invited or accepted **Friend** requests from. This term can be used in reference to other platforms as well.
Get Your ASK in Gear	Inspired by Debbie Allen, **Get your ASK in Gear** is a reminder that you need to Ask questions in order to achieve results.
Grace	A character in *Evict the Bully in Your Head*.

Group Tasking	Combining activities together that require the same resources, to get them done quicker and more efficiently. See the **Rock Star Guide to Gettin' It Done** for the step-by-step format to achieve success.
Gushing	**Gushing** is the oversharing that happens when people are excited about their products, services or business and they have not yet learned the art of **BYT**. It is usually the first sign that someone is infected with **TMI Syndrome.**
Habit Train	The fastest, most efficient way to travel around **Success Island**. Its railcars include: **Planning, Systems, Procedures, Schedules, Routines, Efficiency** and **Productivity**, and the conductor is **Auto Pilot.**
High Tech	Utilizing technology to allow us to be more efficient with our time and resources. **High Tech** allows us to be **High Touch.**
High Touch	Setting yourself apart from others by using your personal touch to connect with your contacts.
Hobbyist	Someone who gets into the industry to get a discount on their own products to subsidize their hobby.
Hope	A character in *Evict the Bully in Your Head*.
Hope Helo	A mode of transportation throughout **Fitchipelago**.
Hope Island	An island in **Fitchipelago** that you will be visiting during the **#12Books12Months** series.
How Can I? (HCI)	The magic question that engages the brain's autonomic response into actively solving the question or problem at hand. It is the replacement phrase for "I Can't."
Human to Human #H2H	Best Selling author Bryan Kramer's description of the way we now do business.

Imposter Syndrome	Feeling like you are a fraud or experiencing the **FEAR** that others will think you are.
Just out of curiosity…	The magical phrase to help you on your entrepreneurial journey.
K.I.S.S.	**K**eep **I**t **S**imple **S**weetheart. My **PMA** version of the original phrase.
KLT Factor	**K**now, **L**ike & **T**rust Factor. Your goal is to develop the **KLT** with your clients, customers, **Followers**, and **Fans** as quickly as possible. People do business with those they **Know, Like, & Trust**.
Know, Like & Trust (KLT)	The **Know, Like, & Trust** Factor is what people seek before they will do business with you. They need to KNOW who you are, LIKE what you represent, and TRUST that you are honest and full of integrity.
Layering	**Layering** is the process of engaging in multiple activities simultaneously without diluting your **Efficiency** in any of them.
Lens	Your **Lens** is a compilation of your journey through life. In essence, it is your "reality" and how you see the world.
Like	A positive **Social Media** response to your content.
Livestreaming	**Livestreaming** is the act of streaming live. Therefore, in my opinion it is a VERB, an action word. I have chosen to use it that way throughout most of what I write and until the mainstream catches up, it is a **Fitchism**.
Love	A character in *Evict the Bully in Your Head*.
LTV—Lifetime Value	**Lifetime Value** of a Customer. (also referred to as CLV, CLTV, or LCV.) is the revenue generated during the life cycle of the customer.

Lunch n Learns	An event where you bring your products and services in during a lunch period, so you can speak to a larger group of people. It usually involves you providing lunch.
Lurkers	A large group of people on **Social Media** who are often watching, but rarely participating.
M3	**M3** or M Cubed stands for **Money, Mindset & Motivation** and is the Philosophy that I run my life and my business by.
M3 Philosophy	My Philosophy, that well-rounded growth for an entrepreneur, is created from a healthy balance between the 3 areas of **Money, Mindset & Motivation**.
M3 Triangle	It is similar to the Bermuda Triangle, but this is a place where instead of getting lost, you get found. You find the most authentic, best version of yourself that has been hiding from the **Bully in Your Head**.
Make your Move	This is the physical act of engaging in specific movement or sequence of movements, which is designed to trigger a change in your current thinking pattern. This is a Tony Robbins suggested activity that is extremely successful in what Tony calls, "Changing your State." (As in changing your state of mind.)
Market Separator	The specialty thing you do, give, or provide that separates you from everyone else who does what you do.
Marauder	Someone who steals or attacks, raids or plunders.
Midnight Madness	An event that encompasses the hour of Midnight.
Mini Marauder	Someone who chooses to be inauthentic to try to gain social traction instead of putting in the work to create authentic engagement.
Mobile Classroom	See **University on Wheels**.

Momentum	The coal that keeps the **Habit Train** moving.
Naysayers	**Naysayers** are the people in your life who continue to discourage your ideas, talents and abilities and tend to be the catalyst for birthing the **Bully in Your Head.** These people are often friends or family members that have a lack of vision or lack of **Confidence** in themselves.
NCT	**New Consultant Training**—The training that new team members should go through to learn about your business. This training should provide the tracks for the **Habit Train** to run on, so they can develop into **Experts** in your industry and capable leaders on your team.
Newsfeed	The steady stream of information that shows up on your **Social Media** channels.
No-Brainer	Something that is obvious and requires little or no thought to make the decision.
Non- Negotiables	Those items in your life that are of the utmost importance; or the items that cannot be changed due to outside circumstances or due to your unwavering commitment to them. The term is used particularly when setting your **Schedule** and is a building block in the **Rock Star Guide to Gettin' It Done.**
Nooks & Crannies	All the available spaces and places.
Not Valley	A location on **'Nough Nation.**
Nudge	The tiniest, and sometimes unnoticeable, change in trajectory that keeps you from ending up at your desired destination.
Obvious to Outlandish	My way of giving you freedom to allow your mind the opportunity to explore possibilities. When being a **Problem Solver**, even the Outlandish ideas can lead you to the perfect solution.

Ocean of Overwhelm	A place off the coast of **Fitchslap Island** where people who are overwhelmed get stuck and immobilized.
One & Done	The missed opportunity, when only one sales is made to a client, because no one followed up or built a relationship with them.
Overcoming Objections	The process of **Peeling the Onion** to uncover the true **FEAR** or objection that is holding them back, so you can help them resolve it.
Pain of Perfectionism	The agony of always falling short of **Perfectionism** and believing the lie that you are Not Enough the way you are. **#YouAreEnough**
Pain of Perfectionism Peaks	A place on **Success Island** where some entrepreneurs get stranded while pursuing a way to do things "perfectly".
Pain Point	An area of concern or difficulty for a person, family, group, or business. It may be something they are acutely aware of and need to solve, and it may be a problem that hasn't been recognized yet. Solving **Pain Points** is the primary objective in selling your products and services.
Peeling the Onion	The act of identifying the real concern that is preventing the client from moving forward. **Peeling the Onion** refers to gently removing each layer until you find that which is truly troubling or causing discomfort.
Perfection	A character in *Evict the Bully in Your Head*.
Persistence	A character in *Evict the Bully in Your Head*.
Pinnacle of Peace	The most coveted place on all of **Success Island**. It is located on the top of **#RockThatDream** Ridge.
Planning	A railcar on the **Habit Train**.

PMA	**PMA** stands for **Positive Mental Attitude**. It is the act of **choosing** to look at the **Bright Side** of things and keeping your attitude and actions in check, while always focusing on the positive possibilities.
Positive Mental Attitude	See **PMA**
Problem Identifier (PI)	Someone who notices everything that is wrong and then dumps it on someone else to resolve.
Problem Solver (PS)	Someone who looks at their problems with optimism and a commitment to finding a solution. **Problem Solvers** always look for at least 3 possible solutions.
Procedures	A railcar on the **Habit Train**.
Productivity	A railcar on the **Habit Train**.
Profit in the Pain	A way of looking at your circumstances while recognizing that even in the midst of what is happening, someday you will find Profit (something positive) in the situation. It is also the title of one of the books in the **#12Books12Months** series.
Pull Up Your Bootstraps	It means to prepare yourself for a situation or a piece of information you might not like. This statement is often made right before a **#Fitchslap**, a **#TruthBomb** or something that might catch the participant off guard. **#PUYB**
Queen of Consistency	A title given to me by my team, due to the **Consistency** in my **Schedule** and activities.
Quit your Fitchin' (#QYF)	A term that means to stop complaining and to get your attitude right. After being told to **Quit Your Fitchin'**, one should immediately look for the **Bright Side** and start moving themselves toward a **PMA**.
Quit your Fitchin' Cave	A place on **Fitchslap Island** where many of the **Problem Identifiers** hang out together.

Raving Fans	**Fans** that sing your praises to others and rave about your products and/or services.
Reassurance Reef	A gorgeous reef off the west side of **Success Island** with warm waters that are gentle and reassuring.
Recruiting Road	The fastest, easiest way to get to #**RockThatDream Ridge**.
Reduce it to the Ridiculous	A Tom Hopkins phrase that means to take what you need to do, and break it into bite sized pieces, that are more easily executed.
Reframe, Reframed, Reframing	To look at something with a different perspective or by applying a different **Filter**. It often requires the concentrated effort of **Empathy** for another person or situation.
Rejection Ridge	A place that is feared because of its name. The ridge looks scary from one side, but there is a soft slope that leads right to **Recruiting Road**.
Rewards Chart	A chart that includes the rewards to be earned for different accomplishments in your business.
Rock Star	A Rock Star is someone who doesn't follow rules, they make their own. They go out of their way to be extraordinary, different from everyone else.
Rock Star Guide to Gettin' It Done	The Step-by-Step Organization & Execution System designed to help you get MORE done in LESS time. *"It will change your life… if you let it."*
Rock Star Referrals	Exceptional referrals that are based on the relationships and excellent reputation you've built for yourself.
Routines	A railcar on the **Habit Train**.
RSG2GID	The abbreviation for the **Rock Star Guide to Gettin' It Done**.
Sales Street	A thoroughfare on **Success Island**.

Salesy Shore	A place people get washed up on **Fitchslap Island** when they use **Sales, Sleazy or Cheesy** tactics.
Salesy, Sleazy & Cheesy	Negative terms that are often applied to people who are in sales or are on a mission to sell you something without regard for your needs. (Although Salesy & Sleazy were terms I used often, shout out to Kimra Luna who added Cheesy into the mix as a third alternative in describing these unfortunate sales **Experiences**. In *DS401* we will talk about marketing and why rhyming makes for great branding!)
Schedules	A railcar on the **Habit Train**.
Scouts	People you reward for "scouting out" other talent or prospects for your business.
Sea of Mediocrity	One of the **Sister Seas**, The **Sea of Mediocrity** is a place where people who lack vision and ideas float along aimlessly, without commitment or dedication. They get by with the minimum effort required.
Sea of Sameness	Another of the **Sister Seas,** the **Sea of Sameness** is a place people go when they refuse to *Step Up & Stand Out*. Their entire purpose is to seamlessly blend in and never be singled out, lest someone actually have an **Expectation** that they can be more than they are. This is where the average person gets stuck as the **Tide of Temptation** drags them away from reaching their **Dreams**. Everyone and everything here looks and acts exactly the same. #NoCreativityAllowed

Sea of Status Quo	Nestled between the **Sea of Mediocrity** and the **Sea of Sameness**, you'll find the Middle Sister, the **Sea of the Status Quo**. She desperately wants to keep everything the same. Control is her vice. Everyone travels in the same direction and making waves is forbidden. Any attempt to Rock the Boat and you will be abandoned, destined to be tossed against the rocky reef or to wash up on the shore of **Not Valley**. **#DontRockTheBoat**
Sea of Tranquility	A place off the southwest side of **Success Island** with calm waters that allow for easy navigation.
Selfish Zone	That place where you are under the false delusion that everything is about you.
Serial Entrepreneur	An entrepreneur that establishes a business or enterprise, gets it running smoothly, and then sells it or delegates the responsibilities to a qualified person, so they can repeat the process over again.
Share, Sharing	The practice of sharing out other people's content on **Social Media**.
Sister Seas	The **Sea of Sameness**, **Sea of Status Quo** and **Sea of Mediocrity** create the triad, called the **Sister Seas**.
Slow Painful Death (SPD)	**Slow Painful Death** references the dying of anything that you are not actively investing your energy in. Particularly used to refer to your **Dreams** and the act of committing **Dreamicide**.
SM	Short for **Social Media**.
Social Media	Any new or existing platform that primarily uses social interaction and user generated content on the internet as a way to communicate and connect people together.
SPD	See **Slow Painful Death**.
Stability Shore	The northeastern shore of **Success Island**.

Stepping Stones	When the results of something are less than you anticipated, the **Bully in Your Head** will call it a **Failure,** but that is a lie. It is a **Stepping Stone** that leads you to growth and strength. **#ProfitInThePain**
Stop n Shops	Open House type events where customers come and shop during a specific set of hours. Typically, your products will be on display or packaged in a way that is inviting, thematic or offers some type of specials or gift with purchase.
Success Island	The center of **Fitchipelago** and home to **#RockThatDream Ridge** and the coveted **Pinnacle of Peace.**
Systems	A railcar on the **Habit Train.**
Throw Away Questions	A question that has not been well thought out, is vague, or very commonly used.
Thumbs Up	A **Facebook** specific term that means you **Like** a post or comment.
Tide of Temptation	The **Tide of Temptation** sweeps many people away from reaching **Success Island** and often leaves them floating aimlessly in the **Ocean of Overwhelm.**
Time Saving Twins	**Group Tasking** and **Layering** are also known as the **Time Saving Twins.**
TMI Syndrome	Too Much Information Syndrome (**TMI Syndrome**) is a disease that needs to be eradicated quickly to prevent it from causing permanent damage to your reputation. A **#Fitchslap** is often needed for proper inoculation.
Tongue in Cheek	Something funny that makes a point without really meaning what the words themselves are saying.
Training In Tandem	The act of learning while someone else under your care is learning at the same time.

Tribe	A **Tribe** is a group of people with similar interests, goals or passions. Your **Tribe** is a group of people who enjoy your content and have connected with you to support your efforts.
Trifecta	When your customers **Know, Like & Trust** you, that is the **Trifecta.**
Troll	A **Troll** is someone who intentionally tries to emotionally harm or distract you in the online world. Specifically, those who come into your **Livestream** simply to disrupt it, or to get attention.
T-Vite	**T-Vite** stands for Text Invite, **which** is a visually appealing graphic invitation that can be texted to all the guests.
University on Wheels	Learning "on the go". Listening to books, podcasts, or other content while traveling or engaging in another activity that doesn't require the active part of your brain.
Upline	The person that is sponsoring another person (**Downline**) into the company.
Vanity Metrics	Numbers that relate to **Likes, Comments, Shares, Followers**, etc. and the misguided idea that larger numbers make you more relevant or important.
Vibe with my Tribe	An expression used to suggest that the people who **Follow** you or connect with your mission or message will likely get along with (**Vibe**) with your other supporters (**Tribe**).
Viral	Spreading virally across **Social Media** or getting extensive reach on one specific platform.
Virtual Event	An online event.
VLOG	Similar to a BLOG, a **VLOG** is the video version— Video **BLOG** or Video Log.

Vultures	People in the online space that are out for your money. They may or may not provide great value, but when you are out of money, they are out of time for you, and will kick you to the curb.
Warm Body Syndrome	The desperation of a hostess to have ANYONE in the room, whether they want to be there or not.
Weeds of Wallowing	A place on **Fitchslap Island** where many people get stuck wallowing in their problems.
WIIFM	**What's In It For Me?** The question we must always answer if we want to keep people engaged.

#FITCH5000

NOTE: If you don't see your name here and you are part of the **#Fitch5000**, or if you want to be part of the **Tribe** so your name will show up in future books, go to **www.VickiFitch.com/DS101** and let us know. Remember that the content is submitted long before the book is officially published, so you may be showing up in a later book, but feel free to let us know!

Charter Members

Carmela Mae Acot
Mikayla Rose Alley
Sarah Belle Alley
Iris Aroa
Mary Aurellano
Karen Barrows
Kim Bates
Kelli Beirow
Lisa Benson
April Bowen
Callum Bowen
Dan Bowen
Eliza Bowen

Judah Bowen
Olive Bowen
Dorothy Boyd
Stacy Braiuca
Lise Brake
Ross Brand
Erin Burch
Dean Burt
Suzanne Burt
Nyra Carranza
Erin Cell
Yanna Cerez
Joel Comm

Melissa Compani
Anthony Conklin
Doug Crowe
Diego Dalessandro
Jeremy Dalton
Kira Dawson
Shanon Dean
Stacey DePolo
Wagner Dos Santos
Spike Edwards
Jill Elliott
Lisa Elliott
Irv Federman

Amellali Figueroa

Andrew Fitch

Becky Fitch

Doris Fitch*

Elijah Fitch

Eric Fitch

Erika Fitch

Garrett Fitch

Hudson Fitch

Jack Fitch

Jason Fitch

Jeff Fitch

Justin Fitch

Layton Fitch

Liam Fitch

Lucas Fitch

Michelle Fitch

Olivia Fitch

Palma Fitch

Suzie Fitch

Ted Fitch

Terry Fitch

Zach Fitch

Wanita Fourie

Hanz Freller

Brittney Frewing

Dave Frewing

Jacob Frewing

Janet Frewing

Justin Frewing

Jay Garrett

Bryan Germain

Carolyn Gialamas

Joe Girard

Laurie Goldman

David Gonzales

Joy Gouge

Lyne Goulet

Mike Grear

Henry (HHH) Hainault*

Joan Hainault*

Steve Hainault

David Hancock

Grover Harp

Randall Harp

Stacy Harp

Tug Harp

Dawn Harper

Johnny Harrell

Malia Hassenbien

Mara Hassenbien

TJ Hassenbien

Tom Hassenbien

Tyler Hassenbien

Bryce Heggen

Brynn Heggen

Kamryn Heggen

Kennedy Heggen

Kim Heggen

Rob Heggen

Karla Henry

Cindy Hettinga

Harvey Hettinga

Helene Hettinga

John Hettinga

Pete Hettinga

Debra Hiller

Marsha Hirschhorn

MoniQue Hoffman

Debbie Hogshead

Kathi Hollingsworth

Jim Bob Howard

Tom Iwema

Jenny Jones

Raul Jusino

Adam Kirk

Addie Kirk

Jennifer Kirk

Kendell Kirk

Megan Kirk

Kara Lambert

D Jay Lareno

Amy Lazare

Jeannie Lokey

Brandon Love

Debbie Lovett

Jennifer Lucas

Moonshadow Machado

Gideon Madsen

Josie Madsen

Julien Madsen

Kevin Madsen

Trisha Madsen

Laura Mandzok

Shannon Mattern

Calvin Mattoon

Madison Mattoon

Martin Mattoon

David McCormack

Tom McDowell

Sean McKenna

Jay McKey

Christine Mercado

Maureen Messersmith

Susan Metzger

Adam Migacz

Jennifer Montague

Avery Jean Morales

Adam Nally

Eric Neitzel

Craig Nelson

Peter Nez

Lisa O'Loughlin

David Parsons

Jimmy (James Jr.) Parsons

Pa (James Sr.) Parsons

Shanna Sheerie Parsons

Judy Peacock

Ernie Perry

Victor Pierantoni

Jennifer Quinn

Leisa Reid

Russ Repass

Melissa Rost

Aaron Roth

Anna Rounseville

Ted Rubin

Elis San Jose

Madison Sanders

Wendy Sanders

Claudia Santiago

Drew Sasser

Kiki Schirr

Stasia Schmidt

Kelly Schuh

Jackie Schulte

Kevin Schulte

Lexi Schulte

Roy Schulte

Chloe Shannon

Hunter Shannon

Rik Shannon

Riky Shannon

Susan Shannon

Walter Shannon

Karen Shillieto

Frances Shurley

Reddy Kumara Simha

Patricia Sommer

Tiffany Souhrada

Amber St. John

Barry St. John

Brandon St. John

Jan St. John

Jeffrey Stipe

Andrea Stonerook-Nunn

Lisa Sulsenti

Jody Summers

Linda Thierry

Maria Thompson

Eric Thorsell

Kathy Thorsell

Amar Trivedi

Dee Trivedi

Rachael Tupper

Jan Turley

Teresa Velardi

Stevie Lynn Vine

Mia Voss

Ben Warren

Jack Warren

Mitchel Warren

Taylor Warren

Tera Warren

Teri Werner

Claire Williams

Darryl Williams

Harrison Williams

Lydia Williams

Trevor Williams

Melanie Wiser

Rafferty Yao

Jason Zara

*Honoring those who had an impact on this journey, but are not longer with us.

Join the Tribe and get your name in the next books!
www.VickiFitch.com/5K

WHAT'S NEXT...

Order your copy of Book #2 in the Series NOW!
www.VickiFitch.com/ETB

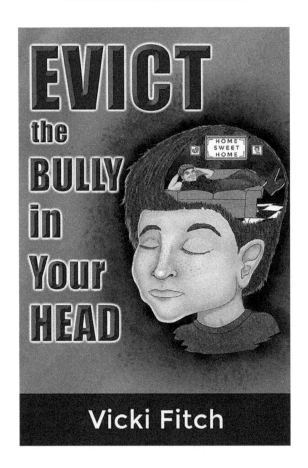

What others are saying about
Evict the Bully in Your Head...

Evict the Bully in Your Head is a cohesive and cogent book that will help everyone change the way they think and act. Vicki examines the numerous Bullies we all deal with and gives step-by-step directions to the Eviction Process. She's taken years of experience of coaching and working with people in business, as well as having a special needs child, and made a fun, informative and life changing book. This book should be required reading for counselors. It uses cognitive behavioral principles but adds a little spice to make it fun for everyone. Highly recommended.

– **Stacy Lynn Harp, M.S.**

Having been blessed enough to choose to be **#Fitchslapped** by Vicki as one of her clients, I have never been more excited to see this book come to press. What you will read in these books is not only the writing of an amazing, ambitious, yet down to earth human being, but one who has a gift from Creator to gently guide others toward their Dreams and help them slay bullies to get there. She not only teaches the talk in this book, but I can firmly attest to her walking the walk in all you read here. As a Clinical Social Worker for over 20 years, I can easily say Vicki and her lessons match, if not exceed, many seasoned therapists I know. I hope you are as blessed as I have been by the lessons and wisdom Vicki brings to this and all of her work.

– **Stacy Braiuca**, MSW, MPH, LCSW, LSCSW,
Entrepreneur/Owner of Braiuca Enterprises, LLC.

ABOUT THE AUTHOR

Vicki started her first business at 12, bought her first house at the age of 19 and started her first company when she was 20. She calls herself a "Serial Entrepreneur" because building and selling businesses became a way of life. She entered the Direct Sales industry over 20 years ago and spent a decade celebrating Top 10 in Sales and Recruiting worldwide, while raising a family, including a child with special needs.

She specializes in helping people of all ages to become the best version of themselves and is passionate about her **#YouAreEnough** campaign to help everyone recognize their value just the way they are. She believes if we start helping children **#EvictTheBully** in their heads, we will build a stronger, more confident generation of leaders that will benefit the future.

Her world recognized speaking and coaching programs have expanded her consulting business to 6 countries across the globe. As a well-rounded entrepreneur that understands all aspects of business, she helps companies to see a greater vision, as well as streamline and automate some of their efforts. She is highly trained in sales funnel automation and explains how to use *"High Tech"* *so you can be* *"High Touch"* to create authentic, long lasting relationships.

Her Weekly Podcasts including *He Said, Red Said* and *Vicki Fitch Live: A Fresh Perspective* were the first to go on Facebook Live and she delivers value daily on Instagram Periscope, Facebook Live and YouTube, training on *"Sales to Social Media & Everything in Between."*

Social Media is one of her strengths and **Livestreaming** is one of her passions. Vicki generated a six figure income in less than 1 year from her live video platforms and created a Free Course called *#RockThatStream* to help others develop their talents in this rapidly emerging area.

Vicki shares a **"Never Give Up!"** philosophy and is empathetic to those who have gone through difficulties since she experienced a multitude of trials herself. Those include losing a baby, losing both of her parents and spending 3 ½ years in a wheelchair. She had to learn to refine her skills and reinvent herself in an online world since she had to spend a significant time in bed. She is often referred to as the **#HopeDealer** because her clients say, *"Working with Vicki is like a drug."* and she reminds her clients that feeling is called **Hope**.

Her love of helping others and contributing to a positive community led her to connect quality entrepreneurs in her Facebook Group, The Entrepreneurial Rock Stars and as a Christian Entrepreneur she and her husband contributed by running a Non-Profit Organization (CYAA-Christian Youth Athletics Association) for over ten years.

Vicki lives in Southern California with her husband Terry of 20+ years and their two boys. She is blessed to also have two amazing step-children who have enriched her life personally and by the five grandchildren they have brought into the world that fill her heart with joy. Her business is her ministry and she believes that it is her opportunity to inspire others through her writing and speaking. God has blessed her greatly and as paraphrased from Luke 12:48… *"To whom much is given… much will be required."* It is her honor to share the message of **Hope** to the world… one book, one **Livestream**, or one event at a time.